The Returned Battle Flags

Edited by Richard Rollins

Rank and File Publications
1995

Preface

The battle flag of the Civil War, both Confederate and Union, played a crucial and transcendent role in combat. It was a primary means of communication in what modern armies call "command and control." Officers and men looked for it to see where a regiment was located, and officers issued commands for maneuver based on its presence. Men followed it, carried it, shot at it, and fought and died for it. In combat the Civil War soldier always looked for it waving overhead.

The Confederate battle flag served as a source of motivation for men on both sides. For Union troops it symbolized the Southern rebellion and their efforts to undermine the freedom and democracy that Union men believed their government embodied. The capture of a Confederate battle flag was an important achievement, symboling individual and/or unit bravery and effectiveness in combat.

To Confederate soldiers, the battle flag was somewhat more complicated. It symbolized all the reasons they were in the army and went into combat. It stood for their defense of their family, home, and community; their efforts to preserve their heritage of freedom and democracy tracing back to the American Revolution, all of which they believed their new nation embodied. To them the flag represented God's will that the Confederacy would survive, but perhaps most of all it represented the men who had fought alongside them and been killed or wounded. For more information on what the flag symbolized and its role in combat, see Richard Rollins, *"The Damned Red Flags of the Rebellion": The Capture of Confederate Battle Flags at Gettysburg* (Redondo Beach, CA: Rank and File Publications, forthcoming).

The Flags Of The Confederate Armies. Returned To The Men Who Bore Them (St. Louis: Charles E. Ware, 1905), is the first item included here. It was originally given by the Cotton Belt Route railroad company to each of the veterans attending the reunion of the United Confederate Veterans at Louisville in 1905. It has never been reprinted, and is considered a rare book, often costing $100 to $300, but usually difficult to find at any price.

As a reading of *The Flags Of The Confederate Armies* reveals, no single dominate pattern of the "Confederate battle flag" ever existed. There were instead a variety of patterns, perhaps as many as 20 different battle flags. The one we are most familiar with, the rectangular red field with a blue St. Andrew's cross outlined in white, and 13 evenly spaced five-pointed white stars, was in fact first carried into combat in the spring of 1864, when Gen. Joseph Johnston, in command of the Army of Tennessee, directed his men to use it. It never flew in the eastern theater, and was a derivative of the Army of Northern Virginia battle flag, a red square with a blue cross, sometimes outlined in white, and 12 or 13 stars, usually not evenly spaced.

The First National pattern, or Stars and Bars, a field of one white stripe between two red, a blue square in the upper left corner "canton" with a circle of from seven to 13 stars, was probably the most widely flown flag. It was used in battle from 1861 until the end of the war, and also widely used on governmental buildings and various headquarters. The Second National pattern, a white field with the square Army of Northern Virginia battle flag in the canton, was also widely used as a battle flag, especially in the west. Several other flags were carried: the Hardee battle flag, a blue field with a white disc; the Polk pattern, a blue field with a red upright cross outlined in white and 13 stars; the Van Dorn pattern, a red field with a yellow half-moon in the upper left and 13 or less spread unevenly; the East Tennessee pattern, a blue field with a white upright cross; the Bragg pattern, a rectangular flag like the Johnston pattern, but with a 6" pink border and 13 six-pointed stars. In addition, early in the war virtually every company raised in the South carried their own unique flags, and many also carried state flags. The Army of Tennessee carried an especially diverse group of flags. When Johnston introduced his pattern in the fall of 1863 and early winter of 1864, one entire division, led by Maj. Gen. Patrick Cleburne, refused to adopt it and insisted on continuing to carry the Hardee pattern. In addition, many other regiments continued to carry First National, and even Polk flags, as evidenced by their capture at Nashville in December, 1864. Truly, no single pattern could be called *the* Confederate battle flag." For more information on the various patterns, see Joseph Crute, *Emblems of Southern Valor* (Louisville: Harmony House, 1990); Devereaux Cannon, *The Flags of the Confederacy: An Illustrated History* (Memphis: St. Luke's Press and Broadfoot Publishing, 1988); Greg Biggs, *The Handbook of Confederate Battle Flags* (Redondo Beach, CA: Rank and File Publications, forthcoming); Howard Madaus and Robert Needham, *The Battle Flags of the Army of Tennessee* (Milwaukee: The Milwaukee Museum, 1976), and Alan K. Summrall, *Battle Flags of Texans in the Confederacy* (Dallas: Eakin Press, 1994).

The diversity of Confederate battle flags is indicated in a count of the types that appear in *The Flags of the Confederate Armies*. Of the 72 flags gracing its pages over half, 37, are Army of Northern Virginia patterns. There are nine First Nationals; five each of the Johnston and Second National patterns; four state flags; three of the South Carolina-Georgia-Florida pattern; three that are so ragged that they can not be categorized and three that are classified as "other" (the Chief of Engineers flag, for example). Two unique local flags, two of the Hardee pattern, and a single East Tennessee pattern are also included. There are at least 11, and possibly 13, different patterns represented here.

During the war no specific order was given governing the disposition of Confederate flags captured by Union forces. In the majority of cases, but not always, the captor turned turned the flag over to his regimental commander, who then passed it up the line through brigade, division, corps and army command. There are records of some cases in which the captor kept the flag as a trophy of war.

When flags were turned in during the war they were usually accompanied by a scrap of paper or cloth on which was written various details about their capture. When, where and by whom they were captured was often but not always recorded. By 1865 over 500 captured Confederate battle flags were in the possession of the Adjutant General's office in Washington. Unfortunately, many of the notes that were originally turned in were lost sometime between 1865 and 1905. At least 22 were given away by various Secretaries of War with little or no documentation of the gift.

In 1867 the Superintendent of the War Department building, apparently without authorization, had the flags moved into his office, where they were placed in boxes and pigeonholes. In 1875 some of the flags were moved the Ordnance Museum. In 1882 the Secretary of War ordered the flags moved to the basement of the War, State and Navy building, and there they lay, "decaying rapidly."

In 1887 the Adjutant-General suggested that they be returned to the former Confederate states as a gesture of good will and reconciliation. This was put before President Grover Cleveland, who agreed, and issued an executive order giving them back. A hue and cry arose, primarily from veterans' organizations and certain politicians, and Cleveland rescinded the order. Again, there they lay, mouldering and decaying.

Finally, in 1905 the U.S. government sent them back to the Governors of each former Confederate state, as well as the border states. In an effort to determine who would get what, the Adjutant-General's office spent considerable time compiling a hand written inventory of each flag, and added as much information as they could develop about its capture.

That inventory, "Record of Rebel Flags Captured By Union Troops Since April 19, 1861," is the second item included here. A few points of information need to be provided. The clerk who originally compiled the information included his or her initials: thus C., W.W., etc., appear at the end of each entry. Information was added as it developed, so it appears that two or more clerks wrote on a given entry, even though only one recorded his or her initials. The information added later—most importantly the dates that the flags were returned, and sometimes late identification of a flag, is printed here in *italics*. The "Record" was clearly compiled as a tool to be used in the return of the flags, not for publication, thus little attention was paid to spelling and punctuation. We have preserved its errors and omissions. The name of the captor of the flag is usually underlined. George Custer's surname is spelled Custar. At the end of most entries is an italicized and underlined number indicating someone's final count of the Confederate battle flags on the list. Some of the flags carried slogans, and these are usually contained in quotation marks or in smaller print. The "Ord. office" refers to the location of the flag in 1905. The first number of each entry is the official War Department number assigned during or shortly after the war, and was usually stenciled in black on the flag, frequently on the border.

The "Record" contains details about 514 Confederate battle flags. A total of about 1,500 still exist. In addition to the ones returned in 1905, other flags ended up in local museums, such as the Confederate Relic Room in Charleston and Confederate Memorial Hall in New Orleans. Some wound up with organizations such as the United Daughters of the Confederacy in Austin, Texas, and still others in private collections. Those flags that could not be identified in 1905 were given to the Confederate Memorial Literary Society in Richmond, and are presently in the Museum of the Confederacy, along with the Virginia flags. They own over 500 Confederate flags. In addition, the states of Iowa, Minnesota, New York and Wisconsin, and the Chicago Historical Society still retain possession of some flags. No one has compiled a list of all the flags in existence, though a leading scholar, Howard Madaus, has collected a vast amount information and is planning on publishing a three volume set of books, tentatively called *The Southern Cross*.

The vast majority of Confederate flags still extant have not been preserved. Active preservation programs are currently underway at the Museum of the Confederacy, Confederate Memorial Hall, the Alabama State Archives, and the Kentucky Historical Society. It is a delicate, costly, and time-consuming process. All donations will be welcomed.

Richard Rollins
March 28, 1995
Redondo Beach, California

THE FLAGS

OF THE

Confederate Armies.

RETURNED TO THE MEN WHO BORE THEM

BY THE

UNITED STATES GOVERNMENT.

1905.

DESIGNED, ENGRAVED AND PRINTED
BY BUXTON & SKINNER, ST. LOUIS.

COMPLIMENTS
General Passenger Department
J. N. FLANAGAN, G. P. & T. A.,
TYLER, **TEXAS.**

SOUVENIR.

Presented to the Confederate Veterans at their
Reunion, at Louisville, Ky., June 14th, 1905,
with the compliments of the Passenger
Department, "Cotton Belt Route."

"THE RETURNED BATTLE FLAGS."

By Mrs. Eron Opha Gregory
Assistant in Mississippi Department of Archives and History.

Oh, not with gayly spreading folds,
　　And colors fresh and bright,
They fling their gleaming stars and bars,
　　Triumphant, to the light;

But sadly 'round their broken staffs,
　　They droop in faded folds,
Their service o'er, their duty done,
　　Their wondrous story told.

Upon their wreck the warrior aged,
　　Looks long, with moistened eye,
Caressing each worn fold, the while
　　Is heard his heavy sigh.

Once more he sees the gleaming host,
　　That pressed with fearless tread,
Toward the heights of liberty,
　　Strewn with its countless dead.

And never pennon streamed above
　　A rank, more fair than the
Bright ensigns of that proud gray host
　　Of Robert Edmund Lee.

To-day, with flowers springing where
　　War's crimson currents ran,
And peace and love starring all the
　　Rich splendor of the land,

These furled and silent banners stir
　　No sad regret and pain,
For we read our fairest history in
　　The story of their fame.

Returned Arkansas Confederate Flags.

The following historical record of the troops from the State of Arkansas, whose returned battle flags are reproduced as they now appear, faded and battle-scarred, is as complete as it has been possible to make it, much of the material having to be obtained from the memory of old veterans, there being no existing complete records.

Lyons' Regiment—Sixth Arkansas Volunteers. Commenced the war with the following Field and Staff Officers: Richard Lyons, Colonel; A. T. Hawthorn, Lieutenant-Colonel; D. L. Kilgore, Major; C. A. Bridewell, Adjutant; J. F. Ritchie, Quartermaster-Sergeant.

Company "A"—The Capital Guards, of Little Rock: Gordon N. Peay, Captain; John E. Reardon, First Lieutenant; D. C. Fulton, Second Lieutenant; John B. Lockman Third Lieutenant.

Company "B"—The Yellow Jackets, from Calhoun County: Philip H. Echols, Captain; C. A. Bridewell, First Lieutenant.

Battle Flag of the "Bloody" 7th Arkansas Infantry Regiment.
Surrendered at Bentonville, March 19th, 1865. One of the last battles of the war.

Company "C"—From Dallas County: F. J. Cameron, Captain, subsequently becoming Lieutenant-Colonel of the regiment; M. M. Duffie, First Lieutenant.

Company "D"—From Ouachita County: Captain Hodnet.

Company "E"—From Arkansas County: Samuel G. Smith, Captain, subsequently becoming Colonel of the regiment.

Company "F"—From Lafayette County: Samuel H. Dill, Captain.

Company "G"—From Columbia County: D. L. Kilgore, Captain; J. W. Austin, First Lieutenant; N. J. Gantt Second Lieutenant; Thomas Seay, Third Lieutenant; —— Nations, First Sergeant; James H. Paschal, First Corporal, afterwards Orderly Sergeant on re-organization; —— Crown, Second Corporal. On Captain Kilgore becoming Major of the regiment, J. W. Austen became Captain.

Company "H"—From Camden County: Captain Richard Lyons, but on his being elected Colonel of the regiment, Sam H. Southerland became Captain; E. W. Elliott, First Lieutenant; A. J. Griggs, Second Lieutenant; G. A. Proctor, Orderly Sergeant; 7 other officers and 57 men, total of company 69.

Company "I"—From Ouachita County: J. W. Kingwell, Captain; J. H. Scroggins, First Lieutenant; E. N. Hill, Second Lieutenant; J. C. Croxton, Third Lieutenant; H. T. Jones, First Sergeant; H. L. Grayson, Second Sergeant; C. C. Arnold, Third Sergeant; J. A. Thompson, Fourth Sergeant; 4 other officers, 58 men, total strength of company 70.

Company "K"—Captain Barnes; Judge Joseph W. Martin became Captain on the re-organization.

The strength of the regiment on organization was over 1,000 men.

Battle Flag of the 8th Arkansas Infantry Regiment.

Carried through the war and surrendered with Johnson's Army, April 26th, 1865. Also Battle Flag of the 19th Arkansas Infantry Regiment, which was consolidated with the 8th Arkansas Regiment.

Colonel Richard Lyons was killed at the Tennessee River, October 10,1861, and Lieutenant-Colonel A. T. Hawthorn became Colonel of the regiment. Gordon N. Peay, Captain of Company "A" was made Lieutenant-Colonel; First Lieutenant John E. Reardon became Captain of Company "A" and John G. Fletcher was elected from the ranks, First Lieutenant of the company.

After the battle of Shiloh the regiment was re-organized, and Lieutenant Fletcher became Captain of Company "A", and served as such to the conclusion of the war. He was wounded and made prisoner at Murfreesboro and remained in prison four months, when he was exchanged.

Major Kilgore served with the regiment until the summer of 1862 when he was transferred to the Trans-Mississippi Department, under General Albert Rust. On reaching the Department he assisted in organizing the Nineteenth Arkansas Infantry, Col. Smead, and was made Major of it.

The Sixth Regiment went first to Pocahontas, Arkansas; from there to Southeast Missouri; then to Columbus, Kentucky; then to Bowling Green, where it was placed in Hindman's Brigade. When Johnston retreated after the fall of Forts Henry and Donaldson, the Sixth Regiment was one of those which covered the retreat to Corinth, Mississippi. It took part in the battle of Shiloh, and lost many men. From Shiloh it went to Corinth and Tupelo, Mississippi, where the regiment was re-organized. From there it was placed in Bragg's Army, and went to Chattanooga; then into Kentucky, where it took part in the battle of Perryville, October 8, 1862, and Murfreesboro, December 31, 1862; January 2, 1865, at Liberty Gap; at Chickamauga, Septemebr 19 and 20, 1863; Missionary Ridge, November 25, 1863; and Franklin, November 30, 1864.

Battle Flag of the 30th Arkansas Infantry.

In all of these battles it lost heavily, and particularly at Shiloh, Murfreesboro and Franklin.

The Sixth Regiment belonged to Hardee's Brigade, afterwards Lidell's, and then Govan's, and was in Cleburn's Division. It was in General Joseph E. Johnston's army, and took part in all the battles of his campaign opposing Sherman, and finally was surrendered with Johnston at the end of the struggle.

The Seventh Arkansas Infantry was mustered into the Confederate Army with the following field and staff officers: Robert G. Shaver, Colonel; William R. Cain, Lieutenant-Colonel at organization, but afterwards John M. Dean, became Lieutenant-Colonel; James J. Martin, Major,; Jack Horn, Adjutant; H. C. Tunsell, Sergeant-Major; William Atillo, Quartermaster; John D. Spriggs, Commissary; Ben Adler, Wagonmaster; Jenifer T. Spriggs, Ordinance-Sergeant.

The different companies of the regiment were commanded by John C. McCauley, of White County, Senior Captain; George B. Orme, of Jackson County, Second Senior Captain; Joseph H. Martin, of Randolph County, Third Senior Captain; and Captains —— Deason, of Izard County; M. Van Shaver, of Fulton County; John H. Dye, of the "Pike Guards"; —— Warner, of Lawrence County; Wm. Blackburn, of Marion County; —— Mellon, of Randolph County; and —— Brightwell, of Independence County.

The regiment was organized at Smithville, Lawrence County, June 16, 1861; went into camp at Camp Shaver, near Pocahontas, Randolph County, with 1,250 men on the muster rolls. It was the first regiment drilled and disciplined by General Hardee, after its transfer to the Confederate service, and was the nucleus on which he formed his First Brigade, which consisted of the Second and Third Confederate; the Fifth, Sixth, Seventh and Eighth Arkansas Regiments, and McCarver's Regiment, with McCown's Battery.

The Seventh Regiment was in the battles of Shiloh, April 6 and 7, 1862; Perryville, Kentucky, October 8, 1862; Murfreesboro, December 31, 1862 and January 2, 1863; Chickamauga, September 19,and 20, 1863; Missionary Ridge, November 23, 24 and 25, 1863; Ringgold Gap, November 27, 1863; Resaca, May 29, 1864; Pickett's Mill, May 26, 1864; New Hope Church, May 29, 1864; Kennesaw Mountain, June 17 to July 3, 1864; Peach Tree Creek, July 20, 1864; Atlanta, July 22 and 28, 1864; Ezra Church, July 28, 1864; Jonesboro, August 31, 1864; Franklin, November 30, 1864; Nashville, December 15, 1864; and Bentonville, the last battle of the war, March 19, 1865.

At Shiloh the regiment earned the sobriquet of "The Bloody Seventh" bestowed upon them by General Hardee, in person on the battlefield, for their gallant storming of Prentiss' lines, causing him to surrender, and by this name they were ever afterwards known.

There was not a battle nor a skirmish by the Army of Tennessee, but that they bore in it their full share.

The Seventh Arkansas Regiment, (Col. Shavers) had become so decimated from its losses that it was consolidated with the Sixth. After the battle of Franklin, at roll call, only 45 men answered to their names out of the two regiments combined.

At Peach Tree Creek, the regiment was nearly wiped out, and at Bentonville, the Second, Fifth, Sixth, Seventh and Eighth Regiments had become so depleted that they were all consolidated into one regiment, and barely made a good-sized regiment then.

The Seventh went into the war with 1,250 men on its muster rolls, and came out with 150, of whom probably not more than 100 are now living.

After the evacuation of Corinth, while at Tupelo, Mississippi, Colonel Shaver was transferred to the Trans-Mississippi Department, and in that department raised another regiment, which he commanded to the close of the war.

The Eighth Arkansas Infantry Regiment was raised by William K. Patterson, who was made its Colonel, and who commanded it from its organization, of Jacksonport, in the summer of 1861, to the time of its re-organization at Corinth, Mississippi, late in the spring or early in the summer of 1862.

At the re-organization, John H. Kelley became Colonel; James H. Wilson, of Jacksonport, Lieutenant-Colonel; G. F. Baucum, Major. During the Kentucky campaign, Lieutenant-Colonel Wilson resigned; Major G. F. Baucum, became Lieutenant-Colonel; and Anderson Watkins, son of Judge George C. Watkins, Major. Afterwards Colonel Kelley was promoted to Brigadier-General; G. F. Baucum became Colonel; and Anderson Watkins Lieutenant-Colonel.

The regiment was in the battle of Shiloh; then went with Bragg's Army on his campaign in Kentucky; was in the battles at Perryville and Murfreesboro; from there went to Chattanooga; was in the battles of Chickamauga, Missionary Ridge, Ringgold Gap, Resaca, Kennesaw Mountain, Peach Tree Creek, Ezra Church and Atlanta. In this battle Colonel Baucum was wounded, Lieutenant-Colonel Anderson Watkins was killed, and the regiment suffered greatly in killed and wounded, Colonel Baucum was never able to rejoin the regiment after being wounded.

This regiment was one of Cleburne's Division, and participated in all the marches and battles of that command, and surrendered with Joseph E. Johnston's troops, April 26, 1865.

The Eighth Arkansas Infantry entered the Confederate service with the following field officers: Wm. K. Patterson, Colonel; Henry M. Crouch, Lieutenant-Colonel; John A. Price, Major; Dr. L. H. Dickson, Surgeon; Dr. Gee, Assistant Surgeon; and Tom Watson, Quartermaster.

The Nineteenth Arkansas Infantry was organized at Nashville, Arkansas, in November 1861, with the following officers: C. L. Dawson, Colonel; P. R. Smith, Lieutenant-Colonel; Joseph H Anderson, Major; A. S. Hutchinson, Adjutant.

COMPANY "A"—Captain Castleman.
COMPANY "B"—Captain Gabe Stewart.
COMPANY "C"—Captain Spars.
COMPANY "D"—Captain J. H. Carter.
COMPANY "E"—Captain Nathan Eldrigde.
COMPANY "F"—Captain D. H. Hamiter.
COMPANY "G"—Captain D. C. Cowling, afterwards Captain George M. Clark, after the capture of Arkansas Post.
COMPANY "H"—Captain Featherston.
COMPANY "I "—Captain Burton H. Kinsworthy.
COMPANY "K"—Captain Herndon.

The regiment took part in the battles of Elkhorn, March 7, 1862, and Arkansas Post, January 11, 1863.

At the capture of Arkansas Post, about one-half only of the regiment was made prisoners, the remaining portion not being of the garrison. The portion which was captured was taken to northern prisons, and the men were exchanged at City Point, Virginia, in May 1863. After being exchanged, they were consolidated with a portion of the Twenty-fourth Arkansas, Colonel Portlock's Regiment, which had likewise been made prisoners. This new regiment went through the battles of Chickamauga, September 19 and 20, 1863; Missionary Ridge, November 23 and 25, 1863; in all the battles of the Georgia campaign, from Dalton to the fall of Atlanta; on Hood's raid through Tennessee,·and in all the battles under Joe Johnston, in North Carolina, and surrendered with him, April 26, 1865.

The strength of the regiment at organization was 800 men; at the surrender 300 or 350. Adjutant A. S. Hutchinson eventually became Colonel of the regiment.

That portion of the original Nineteenth which was not captured, was consolidated with a portion of a regiment which had been commanded by Colonel Thomas P. Dockery. The regiment thus formed took a new number.

Thirtieth (Hart's) Infantry Regiment—Afterwards **Rogan's Thirtieth;** Robert A Hart, Colonel; Jos. C. Martin, Major; Jas. W. Rogan, Lieutenant-Colonel.

Thirtieth (McNeil's) Fifth Trans-Mississippi—Afterwards **Hart's Thirtieth Infantry Regiment:** Gaston W. Baldwin, Lieutenant-Colonel; Robert A. Hart, Lieutenant-Colonel; Jos. C. Martin, Major; A. J. McNeill, Colonel; Jas. W. Rogan, Major, Lieutenant-Colonel.

This regiment was in battles at Farmington, Mississippi, May 9, 1862, and Richmond, Kentucky, but records are not complete as to other engagements.

A. T. ELLIS,
Editor, the Arkansas Homestead, Little Rock, Ark.

Battle Flag of the 6th Regiment of Kentucky Volunteers.
Captured at the Battle of Jonesboro, Sept. 1, 1864.

Kentucky.

It was believed, at the commencement of the great Civil strife, notwithstanding the neutrality declaration, that Kentucky would constitute the battle ground of the contending armies and many were the convictions that they would be needed at home and that it was unnecessary for even the most sanguinary to hunt for earlier opportunities to shed his blood than would be furnished in due course of time, ready-made to hand.

Consequently camps were established contiguous to Kentucky and the work of recruiting troops for the Southern army was commenced. Some of the most wealthy and influential citizens of the State spent freely for transportation and supplies and aided in every laudable way the effect to recruit troops for the Southern cause.

On the 20th of September, 1861, Col. Joseph H. Lewis, of Glasgow, Ky., established a Camp at Cave City, a few miles from Glasgow, in Barren County, Ky.; Col. Martin H. Cofer, also had authority to organize a battalion in connection with Major Thomas H. Hays (then Captain of a Company of Kentucky State Guard). Col. Lewis and Col. Cofer, finding that they could not succeed in recruiting either two full regiments or battalions in time for the active operations which were now being inaugurated, agreed, after consultation with the officers, and through them with the men of the several companies, to unite the two battalions in process of formation, and organize a single regiment. Early in November, the tents were pitched together, and on the 19th of that month the organization of the **Sixth Regiment** took place.

Joseph H. Lewis was elected Colonel, Martin H. Cofer, Lieutenant-Colonel, and Thomas H. Hays, Major. On September 30, 1863, Col. Lewis was promoted to the rank of Brigadier-General, and Lieut.-Col. Cofer succeeded to the Colonelcy.

The regiment was composed of ten companies of from seventy to eighty-five strong. In addition to the ten companies first enrolled, a company stationed at Hopkinsville, Ky., commanded by Capt. McKinney, of Logan County, Ky., was ordered by Gen. Albert Sidney Johnston, on November 25th, to report to Col. Lewis, as on detached service, but to be incorporated with the Sixth Infantry. It was accordingly entered upon the records as "Co. L." When re-enforcements were sent to Donelson, this company was sent forward to report at that point and fought there with the Eighth Kentucky Infantry. It was surrendered with the other companies of that command; and though Col. Lewis made an effort, after it was exchanged, to have it report to him, it was never with the Sixth Regiment and soon ceased to be considered a part of it.

This regiment was a part of the famous **First Kentucky Brigade,** better known as the **"Orphan Brigade,"** and this fact alone, to those who know the fighting record of the **"Orphans,"** is evidence that the men of the Sixth saw hard service. The **"Orphans Brigade"** was composed of the Second Kentucky Infantry; Fourth Kentucky Infantry; Fifth Kentucky Infantry; Sixth Kentucky Infantry; Ninth Kentucky Infantry; Byrne's, Graves' and Cobb's Kentucky Batteries, and the First Kentucky Cavalry was also attached to this Brigade, and the men of this regiment were designated "adopted orphans".

The **"Orphan Brigade"** was known as one of the finest brigades in either army. The following extract from an article by Prof. N. S. Shaler, a strong Union man, published in Scribner's Magazine (1890) will show something of the brigade's standing among those who had followed its career: * * "Some years ago I sought carefully to find a body of troops whose ancestors had been for many generations upon our soil, and whose ranks were essentially unmixed with foreigners, or those whose forefathers had been but a short time upon this continent. It proved difficult to find in the Northern armies any command which served the needs of the inquiry which I desired to make. It seemed necessary to consider a force of at least five thousand men in order to avoid the risks which would come from imperfect data. In our Federal army it was the custom to put in the same brigade regiments from different districts, thus commingling commands of pure American blood with those that had a considerable percentage of foreigners or men of foreign parents. I found in my inquiry but one command that satisfied the need of this investigation, and this was the First Brigade of Kentucky troops, in the rebel army." * *

When first recruited, this brigade contained about 5000 men. From the beginning it proved as trustworthy a body of infantry as ever marched or stood in line of battle. Its military record is too long, too varied, to even be summarized here. I will note only one hundred and twenty (120) days of its history in the closing stages of its service. On May 7, 1864, this brigade, then in the army of Gen. Jos. E. Johnston, marched out of Dalton, Ga., 1140 strong, at the beginning of the great retreat upon Atlanta before the army of Sherman. In the subsequent one hundred and twenty days, or until September 3rd, the brigade was almost continuously in action or on the march. In this period the men of the command received 1260 death or hospital wounds, the dead counted as wounds, and but one wound being counted for each visitation of the hospital. At the end of this time there were less than fifty men who had not been wounded during the one hundred and twenty days. There were two hundred and forty men left for duty, and less than ten men deserted.

A search into the history of warlike exploits has failed to show me any endurance to the worst trials of war surpassing this. We must remember that the men of this command were at each stage of their retreat going farther from their firesides. It is easy for men to bear great trials under circumstances of victory. Soldiers of ordinary goodness will stand severe defeats, but to endure the despair which such adverse conditions bring for more than a hundred days demands a moral and physical patience, which, so far as I have learned, has never been excelled in any army.

Gen. Jos. E. Johnston, a trained West Pointer, a veteran of two wars and a native of another State, speaking of the **"Orphan Brigade"** said that they were the finest body of men and soldiers he ever saw in any army anywhere.

One of the prominent Southern journals, referring to Gen. Hood's defeat at Nashville, had this remark: "A correspondent of one of our exchanges writes of the unfortunate disaster at Nashville, and incidentally pays the highest compliment to Lewis' Brigade, then absent, which was never known to falter."

The "Mobile Advertiser and Register" speaking of a certain point of Hood's defense, on the same occasion, remarks: "Troops should have been placed at that point of whom not the slightest doubt existed. Had the Kentucky Brigade been there all would have been safe."

When a large portion of the Brigade, including the Sixth Infantry were captured at Jonesboro they were assured by Gen. Davis, Commanding the Federal troops, that they would be treated with the utmost courtesy, and no insult was offered them by any of the Federal soldiers, nor were they deprived of their watches and other private property as was the custom.

Since the close of the war the following members of the Sixth Infantry have been prominent in the affairs of the State of Nations: General, formerly Colonel, Lewis, was a lawyer of note and served for years as a Judge of the Kentucky Supreme Court. He was noted for his impartiality to all who had dealings with him as an attorney, Judge or private citizen; Col. Cofer was elected as Judge of the Kentucky Supreme Court but died before the end of his term; A. M. Adair, was a successful lawyer and held State and County offices; S. H. Bush, prominent lawyer; John T. Craycroft, U. S. Revenue Officer; Capt. Jno. Davis, State Commissioner of Agriculture, U. S. Revenue Officer, etc.; Charles Dawson, Sheriff of Nelson County; Alec V. Duncan, and Thos. G. Duncan, both successful practicing physicians and business men in Texas; W. W. Franklin, physician, and for years Clerk of Barren County Court; Amos Fox, prominent citizen and business man of Atlanta, Ga.; Capt. Richard P. Finn, Educator, member of Legislature; Thos. M. Goodknight, lawyer, Supt. of Schools of Simpson County, Postmaster of Franklin, Ky., Chief Clerk State Department of Education; Virgil Hewitt, Chief Clerk of State Insurance Bureau, for years Assistant Auditor of State; A. L. Harned, member of Legislature; W. S. B. Hill, U. S. Revenue Officer, for years an officer of the Court of Appeals; Helm Hobbs, U. S. Revenue Officer; Jas. A. Hindman, member of Legislature; Alex Lawson, U. S. Revenue Officer; Jas. M. Lee, member of Legislature; Maj. Geo. W. Maxson, for years an educator and leading Presbyterian minister in the South; Lewis McQuown, prominent lawyer; Wm. L. Mudd, prominent lawyer; J. R. Nantz, Postmaster of Hodgenville, Ky., A. W. Randolph, City Engineer of Louisville, for some years, for sixteen years County Suveyor of Jefferson County; Wm. H. Read, for years Clerk of Allen County Court; Jas. S. Roby, member of Legislature; Capt. Noah Smith, Judge Barren County Court; Jas. A. Smith, Postmaster of Glasgow, Ky.; Capt. William Stanley, lawyer, but almost ever since was one of the leading ministers of the Christian Church; Pat Simms, U. S. Revenue Officer; Jno. L. Stout, Justice of the Peace, prominent business man; Elliott W. Thompson, Justice of the Peace, member of Legislature, for years Assessor of Livingston County, Mo.; Ed. Porter Thompson, State Librarian, private Secretary to Governor Buckner, Superintendent of Public Instruction, Custodian of Public Buildings and Compiler of Confederate Records until his death; Geo. W. Wells, U. S. Revenue Officer; Smith E. Winn, prominent physician and business man of California. There are many others who have made excellent citizens of our State too numerous to mention here.

On the 25th of March, 1905, the Secretary of War had the old regimental flag of the Sixth Infantry returned to the Governor of this State. This flag was returned in accordance with an Act of Congress entitled a "Joint resolution to return to the proper authorities certain Union and Confederate battle flags."

This old flag, a reproduction in colors of which is given above, is made of red and blue flannel, the cross bars of white linen. It is mounted on a hickory limb about five or six feet in length. Printed across the face of the flag are the names of the following battlefields: Shiloh, Vicksburg, Baton Rouge, Chickamauga, Murfreesboro.

This flag was captured at the battle of Jonesboro, Sept. 1, 1864, by the Tenth Michigan Veteran Infantry.

Gov. Beckham has turned the flag over to the Kentucky Historical Society and it has been placed in the room of this Society where it will be carefully preserved.

ED. PORTER THOMPSON, JR.,
Compiler Confederate Records, State of Kentucky.

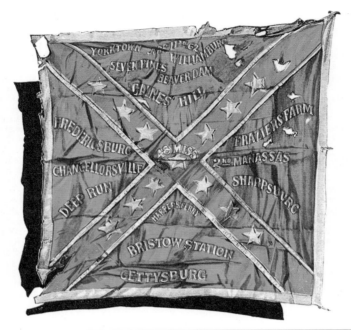

Battle Flag of the 48th Mississippi Regiment.
Date of capture not obtainable.

Mississippi.

Owing to the impossibility of obtaining a full history of the flags returned to the State of Mississippi, only a brief record of the flags reproduced is here given.

Nineteen Confederate battle flags have been returned to the State of Mississippi by the War Department, in carrying out the provisions of the resolution of Congress, and are deposited in the Department of Archives and History where they will be permanently preserved.

Among the most famous of these flags are the Second, Eighteenth and Forty-eighth Infantry, all of which belonged to the Army of Northern Virginia. They represent the regulation battle flag of the Confederacy, and are in a good state of preservation when the rough usage to which they have been subjected is considered.

The battle flag of the **Second Mississippi Regiment** was captured at Gettysburg, and has inscribed on its folds the names of the important battles in which the regiment was engaged, namely: Gaines' Farm, Malvern Hill, Manassas and Seven Pines. This regiment was commanded by Colonels John A. Blair and Bently B. Boon; Lieut.-Col. David W. Humphreys and Lieut.-Col. John M. Buchanan.

The battle flag of the **Eighteenth Mississippi Regiment** is in a good state of preservation. It was captured at Fredericksburg, on the 5th day of May, 1863. This famous regiment took part in all the great battles in which the Army of Northern Virginia was engaged, and was commanded by Col. E. R. Burt and Col. Thomas M. Griffin; Lieut.-Col. W. H. Luse and Lieut.-Col. Walter G. Kearney; Major J. W. Balfour, Major G. B. Gerald and Major E. G. Henry.

The battle flag of the **Forty-eighth Mississippi Regiment** is full of bullet holes and is more tattered and faded than the others. This celebrated regiment took part in the following battles, the names of which almost cover the folds of the flag: Yorktown, Williamsburg, Seven Pines, Beaver Dam, Gains Mills, Frazier's Farm, Second Manassas, Sharpsburg, Harper's Ferry, Bristow Station, Gettysburg, Fredericksburg, Chancellorsville and Deep Run. This regiment was commanded by Joseph M. Jayne, Colonel; Thomas B. Manlove, Lieutenant-Colonel, and L. C. Lee, Major.

In the collection will be found the Eleventh, Fifteenth, two of the Twelfth, Thirty-third, Nineteenth, Sixteenth, Seventeenth, Eighteenth, Sixth, Wigfall Rifles, Fourth, Sweets Battery, First, Forty-second and Forty-fourth. Many of them are still on their original staffs; others are attached to rude poles.

Dunbar Rowland,
State Archivest, Jackson, Miss.

Battle Flag of the 2nd Mississippi Regiment.
Captured at Gettysburg.

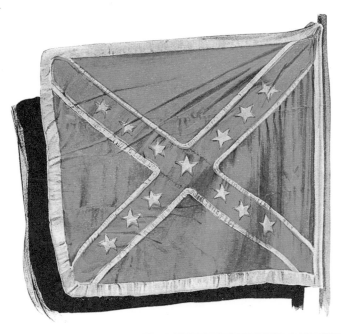

Battle Flag of the 18th Mississippi Regiment.
Captured at Fredericksburg, May 5, 1863.

Flag of Hood's Texas Brigade.
Date of capture unknown.

Texas.

Brief history of the Confederate Battle Flags recently returned by the Secretary of War to the Governor of Texas.

The Flag of the **First Texas Infantry Regiment.** It was captured in the battle of Appomattox, April 8, 1865.

Flag of **Hood's Texas Brigade.** The lower half of this flag is frazzled and tattered. It is a Texas flag in design, and inscribed upon it are the words "Seven Pines," "Malvern Hill" and "Gaines Farm."

The Flag of the **Third Texas Cavalry Regiment.** It was captured in Georgia, August 20, 1864. Upon it is inscribed "Oak Hill," "Holly Springs," "Hatchie Bridge," and "Thompson's Station."

Unknown Flag. It was captured September 17, 1862, It is evidently the flag of a Texas Brigade, but cannot be identified by the public record or by private inquiry.

All these old flags are tattered, battle scarred and bullet riddled, but the colors are as bright as the day upon which they were first unfurled.

HARRY HAYNES,

Austin Statesman, Austin, Texas.

Battle Flag of the 1st Texas Infantry Regiment.
Captured in the Battle of Appomattox, April 8, 1865.

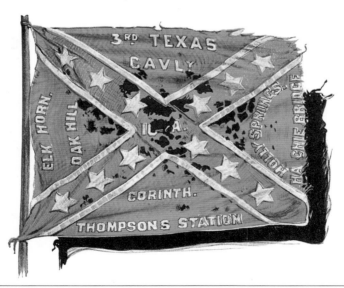

Battle Flag of the 3rd Texas Cavalry Regiment.
Captured in Georgia, August 20, 1864.

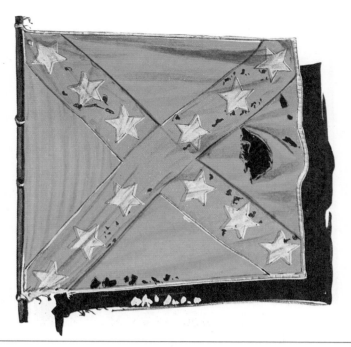

Unknown Flag of a Texas Brigade.
Captured Sept. 17, 1862.

Battle Flag of the 4th Virginia Infantry.
Captured in the Battle of the Wilderness. May 12th, 1864. This regiment
belonged to the famous "Stonewall Brigade."

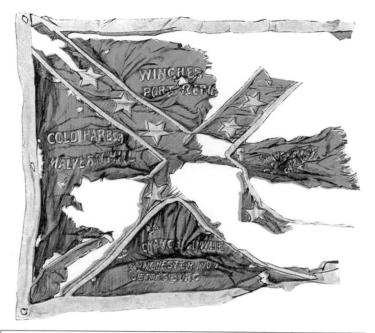

Battle Flag of the 2nd Virginia Infantry.
There is no record of the capture of this flag, but its condition plainly indicates the terrific conflicts through which it passed.

Flags of Virginia.

The return of the battle flags to the Southern States by the Federal Government has been hailed with great joy by the old heroes who wore the gray, and these tattered emblems of more strenuous days are highly prized by those who followed them so devotedly on so many fields.

The Virginia flags returned, are carefully stored away in the Confederate Museum, which was the home of President Davis, during the Civil War. They were shipped from the War Department, each carefully wrapped in a separate package. The box also contained a number of flags on the poles on which they were originally used during the war. The box was placed in the Museum, pending the final decision of Governor Montague as to what disposition he will make of the valued relics, but it is thought the Governor will determine to allow them to remain where they are.

The flags returned to Virginia are indeed interesting. There is, for instance, a flag of the state, made of fine blue silk, which saw service all through the war, and which was presented by the ladies of Bath County. "God Protect the Right" is the inscription.

Another flag of great interest and historic value, is that of the **Second Virginia Infantry.** This old relic went nearly all through the war, and is now but a mere fragment, having been torn almost into shreds by Federal bullets. A picture of this is shown above, and one has but to look upon it to appreciate the service it has seen.

The Fourth Infantry Flag. It was in all the big battles of the famous "**Stonewall Brigade**," and was captured at the battle of the Wilderness, May 12, 1864. It bears an inscription "Rebel Battle Flag", showing also the date of its capture. Upon the flag is lettered the names of the battles through which it passed. These include First and Second Manassas, Winchester, Kearnstown, Harper's Ferry, Cold Harbor, Chancellorsville and Gettysburg.

The flag of the **Forty-seventh Virginia Infantry** is among the very interesting ones. It was captured by the First Michigan Cavalry, at the battle of Falling Waters.

The **Ninth and Forty-eighth Virginia Infantry** flags are both interesting and are highly prized by the old veterans.

The Joint Resolution under which the flags were returned, was offered in the House by Congressman John Lamb, of Richmond, himself a gallant officer in the Third Cavalry, and his old battle flag is distinguished among those returned.

Captain Lamb also drew and offered the report which was adopted along with the resolution.

Only one-fourth of the flag of the **Tenth Virginia Infantry** is left to tell the story of the thrilling battles through which it passed. It was captured at the battle of Sailor's Creek, April 6, 1865, only a few days before the surrender of General Lee's Army at Appomattox C. H. The Tenth Virginia Infantry was a regiment of striking gallantry, and many of its members laid down their lives on the field where their flag was captured.

We give a reproduction of Gen. Jubal A. Early's headquarter's flag. Though soiled and bedraggled by rain, it is in a good state of preservation. It was the marker for the old hero's forces in all his engagements both in the Valley of Virginia and elsewhere, and was carried at the head of his army until the end came. It was with him in Pennsylvania, as well as in all his other engagements throughout the war.

Unknown Flag of Pickett's Corps. This flag was in the major portion of the greatest battles fought by the gallant Gen. George E. Pickett. It is designated as having belonged to **"Pickett's Corps"**, and this of itself is sufficient to mark it at once as an emblem of great historic value. There is no data at hand to show where this flag was captured, though it is evident it waved in the forefront of many fiery engagements.

The flag of the **Thirteenth Virginia Cavalry** is one around which thrilling memories cluster. It was in many engagements both in and out of Virginia, and after having been borne gallantly on many victorious fields, was captured at Hanover, Pa., in July, 1863. The **Thirteenth Virginia Cavalry** was one of the most gallant of all the mounted regiments that followed the fortunes of the Confederacy from Virginia.

Thirty-seventh Virginia Cavalry. This is evidently a flag with an interesting and thrilling history. It is battle scarred and shot and torn into shreds. It is officially designated as the flag of **"Dunn's Battalion, Thirty-seventh Virginia Cavalry"**. It was in many of the most striking engagements of the Valley campaigns and was captured in Luray (Va.) Valley, October 26th, 1864, by the Fourteenth Pennsylvania Cavalry. The flag is quite highly prized and is one of the most interesting of all those returned to Virginia.

Flag of the Engineering Corps, Lee's Army. This flag is of striking appearance and it saw service all through the war, having been carried at the head of the Engineering Corps in blazing the way for some of the most historic battles of the entire struggle. The flag is of extra large size, and is made of red material, the lettering being white, and perfectly distinct. It has also a white border on the side where it was attached to the pole. There is no data to show whether it was captured or simply turned over to the Federal forces at the end of the struggle.

C. A. BOYCE,

Times-Dispatch, Richmond, Va.

Flag of the Engineering Corps, Lee's Army.
No record of its capture.

Unknown Battle Flag of
Pickett's Corps.
No date of capture given.

General Jubal A. Early's Headquarters Flag.
No record of when captured.

Battle Flag of the 9th Virginia Infantry.
There is no date of the capture of this flag.

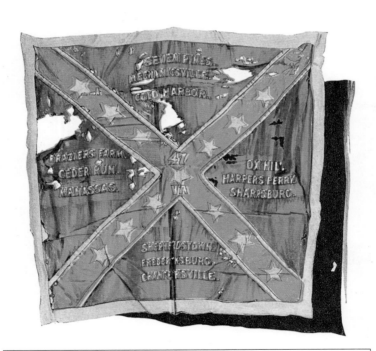

Battle Flag of the 47th Virginia Infantry.
Captured in the Battle of Falling Waters.

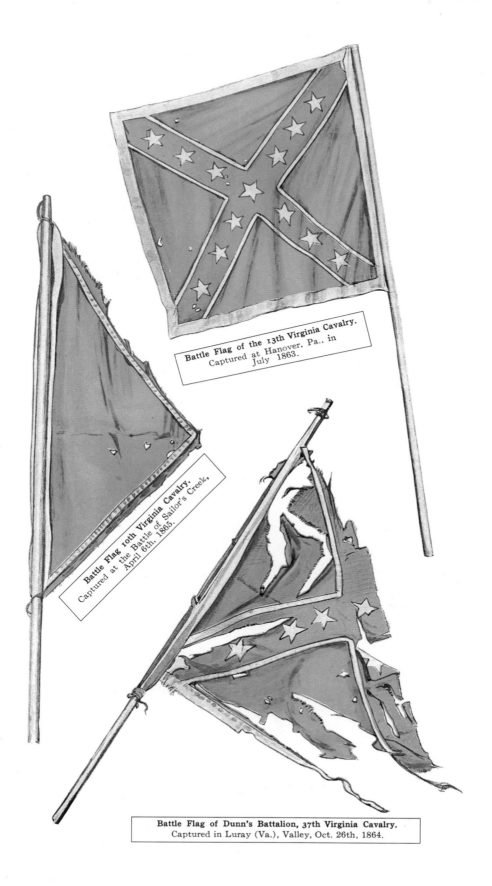

Battle Flag of the 13th Virginia Cavalry.
Captured at Hanover, Pa., in
July 1863.

Battle Flag 10th Virginia Cavalry.
Captured at the Battle of Sailor's Creek,
April 6th, 1865.

Battle Flag of Dunn's Battalion, 37th Virginia Cavalry.
Captured in Luray (Va.), Valley, Oct. 26th, 1864.

Battle Flag of the 48th Virginia Infantry.
There is no date of the capture of this flag.

Company Flag.
Carried by a company raised in Bath County, Virginia.

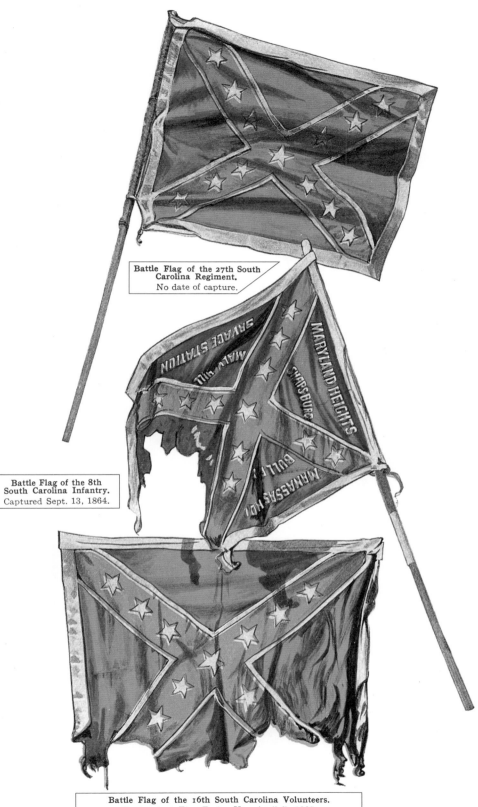

Battle Flag of the 27th South
Carolina Regiment.
No date of capture.

Battle Flag of the 8th
South Carolina Infantry.
Captured Sept. 13, 1864.

Battle Flag of the 16th South Carolina Volunteers.
Captured at Five Forks, Va., April 7, 1865.

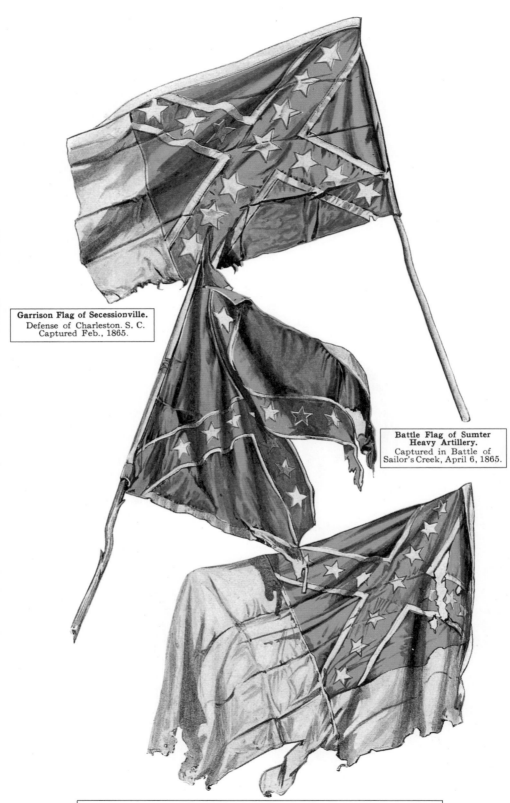

Garrison Flag of Secessionville.
Defense of Charleston. S. C.
Captured Feb., 1865.

Battle Flag of Sumter Heavy Artillery.
Captured in Battle of
Sailor's Creek, April 6, 1865.

Fort Ripley S. C., Garrison Flag.
No record of capture.

South Carolina.

Owing to the fact that many of the Confederate battle flags, returned to the States, were received so very late, and there being no records at the State Capitols of the regiments that bore the flags, it has been impossible to secure information from members of the regiments which carried the flags, and give full histories of them. Particularly is this the case with South Carolina flags, and below we give only a very short history of a few of the South Carolina flags which are reproduced in this souvenir.

Until there is some expression from the Confederate Veterans Association of the State, the battle flags captured during the war, and recently returned to the State by the War Department, are in the keeping of the ladies in charge of the State Relic Room in the Capitol building.

Writing to Governor Heyward, under date of March 25, 1905, Secretary of War Taft, said:

"I have the honor to advise you that, under authority conferred upon the Secretary of War by the joint resolution of Congress approved February 28, 1905, entitled 'A Joint Resolution to return to the proper authorities certain Union and Confederate battle flags,' I have caused to be forwarded to you to-day by express all the Confederate battle flags that were in the custody of the War Department at the time of the approval of said joint resolution, and that could be identified as belonging to your State or as having been borne by military organizations thereof.

"A few of the flags that were described in executive document No. 163, House of Representatives, Fiftieth Congress cannot now be identified. Their numbers or distinguishing marks have been lost, and a few of the flags that could not be identified in 1868 have since been identified and are now returned to the states to which the organizations which bore them belonged."

This "Executive Document" described other South Carolina flags that were captured but Secretary Taft makes no mention of what disposition has been made of them.

A list of the flags returned follows:

Eighth Regiment Infantry.	Fort Moultrie garrison flag.
Eleventh Regiment Infantry.	Citadel garrison flag.
Sixteenth Regiment Infantry.	Secessionville (James Island) garrison flag
Twenty-seventh Regiment Infantry.	Fort Ripley garrison flag.
Castle Pinckney garrison flag.	Three Regimental flags, unidentified.

The only history available, of the several flags returned, is the following:

Eighth South Carolina Infantry Flag, captured Septempber 13, 1864.

Flag of **Eleventh South Carolina Volunteers,** inscribed: "Port Royal, Cedar Creek, Swift Creek, Petersburg, June 24, Weldon Railroad."

Flag of the **Sixteenth South Carolina Volunteers,** was captured during the engagement of April 7, 1865, at Five Forks, Va.

Battle Flag of the **Twenty-seventh South Carolina** Regiment.

Flag of **Sumter Heavy Artillery,** captured in the battle of Sailor's Creek, April 6, 1865.

Garrison Flag of Secessionville, defense of Charleston, captured February, 1865.

Garrison Flag of Citadel, Charleston, S. C., captured February 18, 1865.

Garrison Flag of Fort Moultrie, Charleston Harbor, captured February 18, 1865.

W. H. McCaw,
Columbia, S. C.

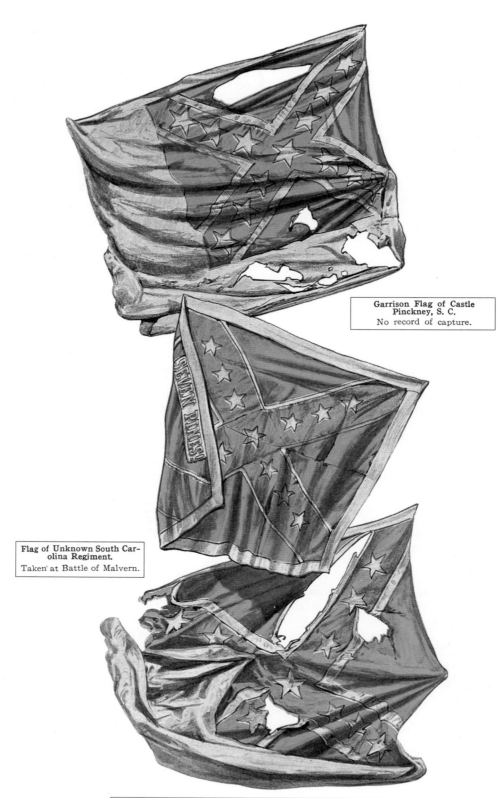

Garrison Flag of Castle Pinckney, S. C.
No record of capture.

Flag of Unknown South Carolina Regiment.
Taken at Battle of Malvern.

Garrison Flag of the Citadel, Charleston, S. C.
Captured Feb. 18th, 1865.

Flag of the 1st Tennessee Battalion.
Captured at the Battle of Chickahominy, July 27th, 1862.

Returned Tennessee Confederate Flags.

The following brief information in regard to the Tennessee Regiments, whose Battle Flags were returned by the U. S. Government, is all that it was possible to obtain in regard to them from the archives on file at Nashville.

First Tennessee Confederate Regiment Battle Flag. It has this inscription, "Confederate Battle Flag of the First Tennessee Regiment, captured at the Battle of Gettysburg, July 3, 1863." The battles inscribed on it are, "Cold Harbor," "Seven Pines,' "Mechanicsville," "Frazier's Farm," "Cedar Run," "Ox Hill," "Harpers Ferry," "Sharpesburg," "Shepherdstown," "Fredericksburg" and "Chancellorsville."

Col. Peter Turney, the Commander of this Regiment, was badly wounded at the Battle of Fredericksburg.

The Flag of the **First Tennessee Battalion,** bears inscription: "Captured at the Battle of Chickahominy, July 27, 1862."

The Sixth Tennessee Infantry. This Flag is inscribed: "Captured at Sailors Creek, April 1st, 1865." The battles in which this regiment was engaged, were Belmont, Shiloh Perryville, Murfreesboro, Tullahoma, Chickamauga, Cat Creek, Dalton, Resaca, Kennesaw, Dead Angle, Peachtree Creek, Atlanta, Jonesboro, Franklin, Nashville, Missionary Ridge and Bentonville.

Geo. C. Porter, was Colonel, W. H. Jones, Lieutenant-Colonel, and J. L. Harris, Major

Flag of the 2nd Regiment East Tennessee Volunteers.
No record of capture

"Colors of the **Seventh Tennessee Regiment.**" This was General Robert Hatton's old Regiment. He was killed at the battle of Seven Pines.

Fourteenth Tennessee Regiment Battle Flag, captured at Gettysburg, July 3, 1863. The battles in which this regiment was engaged were, "Seven Pines, Mechanicsville, Cold Harbor, Frazier's Farm, Cedar Run, Manassas, Ox Hill, Harpers Ferry, Sharpesburg, Shepherdstown, Fredericksburg and Chancellorsville."

This was Col. Forbes' Regiment, he was killed at the second battle of Manassas.

The Battle Flag of the **Twenty-Third Regiment, Tennessee Volunteers:** "Captured, 2d day of April, 1865."

This regiment was consolidated with the Seventeenth Regiment, which was commanded by Col. R. H. Keeble, who was killed at Petersburg, July 31, 1864.

The Flag of the **Forty-Fourth Tennessee Regiment:** "Captured, 17th day of June, 1864, at Petersburg, Va." The battles in which this Regiment was engaged were Shiloh, Perryville, Murfreesboro, Hoover's Gap, Ringold, Chickamauga, Knoxville, Beans Station, Watthall Junction, Drury's Bluff and Petersburg.

Col. John S. Fulton commanded the regiment. He was killed on the 30th day of June, 1864.

This regiment was finally consolidated with the Twenty-Fifth Tennessee, commanded by Col. S. S. Stanton, who was killed at Resaca, Ga., in 1864.

The Second Tennessee Volunteer Regiment Flag. This must have been the Nineteenth Regiment, Tennessee Volunteers.

HARVEY H. HANNAH,
Adjutant General, State of Tennessee.

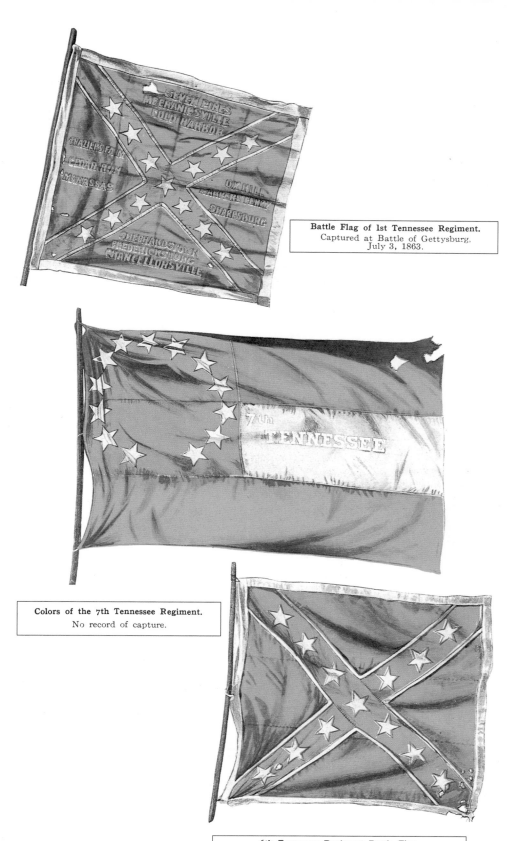

Battle Flag of 1st Tennessee Regiment.
Captured at Battle of Gettysburg,
July 3, 1863.

Colors of the 7th Tennessee Regiment.
No record of capture.

6th Tennessee Regiment Battle Flag.
Captured at Sailor's Creek, April 1, 1865.

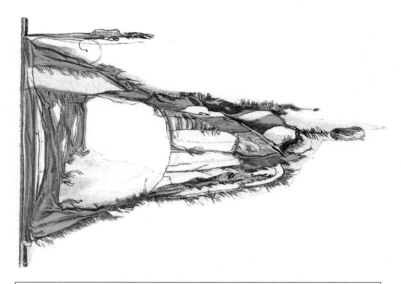

Flag of Unknown Tennessee Regiment.
No record of capture.

Colors of Unknown Regiment of Tennessee Volunteers.
No record of capture.

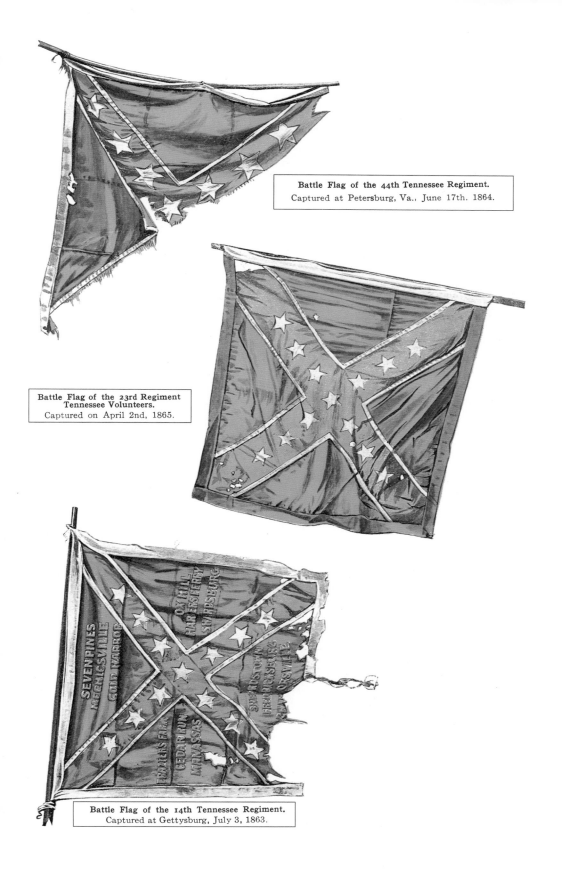

Battle Flag of the 44th Tennessee Regiment.
Captured at Petersburg, Va., June 17th. 1864.

Battle Flag of the 23rd Regiment
Tennessee Volunteers.
Captured on April 2nd, 1865.

Battle Flag of the 14th Tennessee Regiment.
Captured at Gettysburg, July 3, 1863.

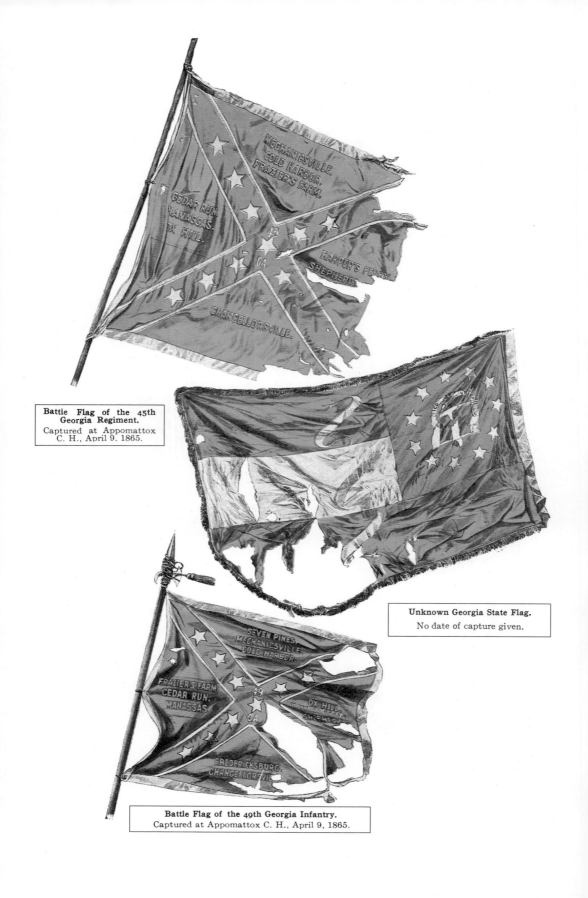

**Battle Flag of the 45th
Georgia Regiment.**
Captured at Appomattox
C. H., April 9, 1865.

Unknown Georgia State Flag.
No date of capture given.

Battle Flag of the 49th Georgia Infantry.
Captured at Appomattox C. H., April 9, 1865.

Confederate Flags of Georgia.

Photographs of twenty-seven flags returned by the Government to the State of Georgia were received, but it was impossible to reproduce more than the fifteen shown in this publication, owing to the shortness of time before the Re-union at Louisville. The history, however, of all of the flags returned to Georgia is given, and if future editions of this publication are issued the other flags will be reproduced.

Flag of the **First Georgia Volunteer Infantry.** This Regiment, commanded by Col. James N. Ramsey, enlisted for twelve months, and organized at Macon, Ga., April 3, 1861; fought in West Virginia under General Robert S. Garnett, taking part in the Laurel Hill engagement, and the fights at Garrick's Fork, Greenbrier River and Cheat Mountain.

In April, 1862, this regiment having served its period of enlistment disbanded. All the companies re-enlisted, however; four Companies forming the **Twelfth Georgia Battalion of Artillery.** Served around Charleston and in the Western Army until June, 1864, when it was armed as infantry and assigned to Gordon's Georgia Brigade, with which it served around Richmond, in the valley, in Early's Maryland campaign, around Petersburg and surrendered at Appomattox.

The other Companies of the First Regiment served in other commands under General Johnston and General Hood in Tennessee, Georgia, and on to Greensboro, N. C., in 1865.

Flag of the **Seventh Georgia Cavalry.** This Regiment was organized in the early part of 1863, served in Georgia and South Carolina until June, 1864, when it joined Hampton's Cavalry in Virginia. Took part in the battle of Trevillian Station, suffering considerable loss, but helped to drive Sheridan back to the Pamunky and defeating his efforts to join General Hunter in his raid against Lynchburg, Va.

This Regiment joined in the fights in the Valley Campaign in 1864, where Early's small Command was overwhelmed by Sheridan.

This flag is one of the latest designs adopted by the Confederate Government. Very few of them were ever used by the Confederate Troops in the field. It was captured by Sheridan's Cavalry, in October, 1864.

Flag of the **Benjamin Infantry.** This Company was one of the Companies of the **Tenth Georgia Regiment,** and this flag was carried to the army when the Company entered the service. When the regiment was organized, and regimental colors given it, this flag was sent back to the County of Clayton, near Atlanta, and was put away in a bureau drawer as a sacred relic. Some soldier, belonging to Sherman's Army, plundered this private residence and carried off the old flag, Kilpatrick having raided in that neighborhood in August, 1864.

Flag of the **Twelfth Georgia Regiment.** This Regiment was first Commanded by Colonel Edward Johnson, and became famous for its heroic services in the Valley of Virginia. When its Colonel became a General, it was commanded by another hero, Edward Willis, and then another, Isaac Hardeman.

It became part of Doles-Cook Brigade of Rodes' Division, Jackson's Corps, taking part in all the battles of Virginia, Maryland and Pennsylvania.

But the flag, purporting to be the flag of the Twelfth Georgia, was not its flag.

Col. James G. Lane, of the One Hundred and Second New York Regiment, claimed in his official report of the battle of Chancellorsville, that his Command captured twenty-three men of the Twelfth Georgia Regiment, including the Color Bearer and his battle flag. Doubtless this New York Regiment captured some prisoners and a flag, but it was not the Twelfth Georgia's Flag. A number of the surviving officers and men of this most gallant Regiment assert most positively that their colors were never lost in battle, either at Chancellorsville or elsewhere during the war.

The Regiment was a part of General Rodes's Division, and Gen. Rodes in his official report of Chancellorsville, mentions the loss of three battle flags by his Division. They were those of the Fifth Alabama, and the Second and Fourth Regiments of North Carolina Troops. The Twelfth Georgia flag was not captured at this place, and was never in any danger of being lost.

Fourteenth Georgia Flag. The Fourteenth Georgia Regiment was one of the Regiments of General E. L. Thomas's Georgia Brigade, A. P. Hill's Division of Jackson's (2d) Corps, afterwards made a part of Third Corps, General A. P. Hill, commanding.

It participated in nearly all the battles in Virginia, Maryland and Pennsylvania and surrendered at Appomattox.

General A. V. Brumby was the first Colonel, succeeded by Colonels Felix Price, Robert W. Folsom and R. P. Lester, in order named.

The flag was probably among those surrendered at Appomattox.

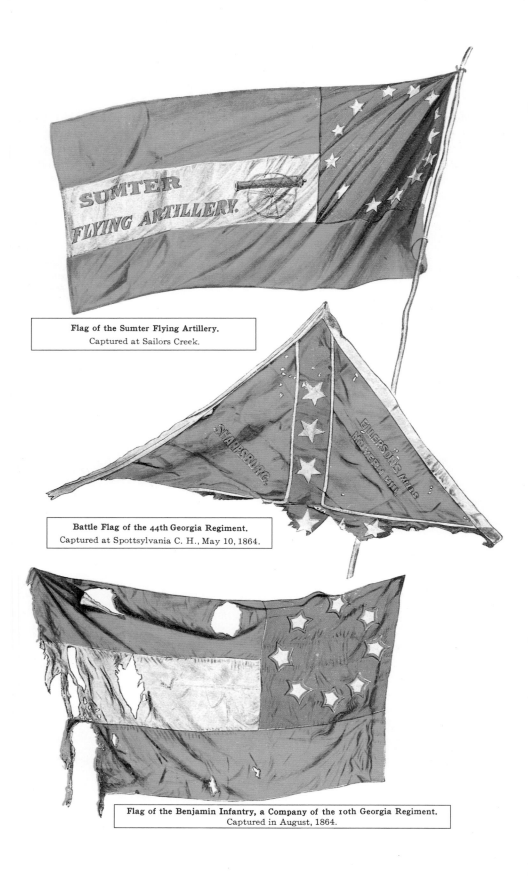

Flag of the Sumter Flying Artillery.
Captured at Sailors Creek.

Battle Flag of the 44th Georgia Regiment.
Captured at Spottsylvania C. H., May 10, 1864.

Flag of the Benjamin Infantry, a Company of the 10th Georgia Regiment.
Captured in August, 1864.

Fifteenth Georgia Regiment Flag. The Fifteenth Georgia was one of the Regiments of General Robert Toombs's Georgia Brigade. After Gen. Toombs's retirement to other fields of duty, the Brigade was commanded by General Henry L. Benning, known by the troops as "Old Rock," companion Brigade to General G. T. Anderson, known as "Old Tige." "Hurry up, Tige, Old Rock has Treed," was the trooper's way of indicating that the latter had located the enemy and needed help.

This Regiment was one of the best in Longstreet's Corps, and fought in the battles in Virginia, Maryland and Pennsylvania, and at Chickamauga and Knoxville. It surrendered with Lee at Appomattox. Col. Thos. W. Thomas was First Colonel, and Judge Linton Stephens, brother of Alexander H. Stephens, was Lieut.-Colonel.

This Regiment's flag was lost at the "Devil's Den," Gettysburg, Pa., July, 1863.

Sixteenth Georgia Regiment Flag. The Sixteenth Georgia was originally commanded by Colonel (afterwards General) Howell Cobb, one of Georgia's most distinguished men.

He had been a member of Congress, Governor of Georgia, Speaker of Federal House of Representatives, and member of President James Buchanan's Cabinet. He commanded a Brigade at Crampton's Gap, Md., where his command was assailed and overwhelmed by several Brigades of McClellan's Army.

The Regiment was afterward one of Wofford's Georgia Brigade. and fought gloriously at Gettysburg, Wilderness, Spottsylvania, around Richmond, Chancellorsville and other battles, and surrendered at Appomattox, crowned with glory although numbered among the vanquished.

Flag of the **Eighteenth Georgia Regiment;** known also as the **"Third Texas,"** by the Texas Regiments of Hood's Old Brigade to which it belonged until 1863, when it was Brigaded with other Georgia Regiments under General W. T. Wofford.

It was one of the most gallant Regiments, and in the fight at Cold Harbor, June, 1864, together with the Fourth Texas Regiment and Hampton's S. C. Legion, charged one mile and captured part of Porter's line with fourteen pieces of artillery and held them. It took part in all the principal battles in Virginia (except Chancellorsville) and in Maryland and Pennsylvania, and surrendered at Appomattox.

Flag of the **Nineteenth Georgia Regiment.** Was one of the Regiments of General Alfred H. Colquitt's Brigade. Took part in nearly all the battles of Virginia and Maryland. Was in the battle of Ocean Pond, or Olustee, Florida, at Fort Sumter, S. C., and helped repulse Grant's assault at Cold Harbor, June 3, 1864, when 7000 Federals were killed and wounded in just twenty minutes by the clock. Later in 1864, Colquitt's Brigade was sent South again to re-enforce Joe Johnston's army before Sherman, and surrendered in North Carolina on April 26, 1865.

Flag of the **Twenty-first Georgia Regiment.** This Regiment has the distinction of sustaining a greater percentage of losses during the four years of service than any other Georgia Regiment. At the second battle of Manassas it lost 64 per cent, killed and wounded, and the remnant held their ground.

It was one of Trimble's Brigade in Jackson's Valley Campaign, taking part in all the engagements against Milroy, Banks, Fremont and Shields. Afterwards became a part of the Doles-Cook Brigade, Rodes' Division, and fought in all the battles in Virginia, Maryland and Pennsylvania. Surrendered fifty men at Appomattox, where the flag was given up. Colonel John T. Mercer, its Colonel, was a West Pointer, and was killed at Plymouth, N. C., when Hoke's Division captured that place.

Flag of the **Twenty-sixth Georgia Regiment.** This Regiment, one of the best fighting Regiments of Gordon's Fighting Georgia Brigade, was commanded by Col. Edmund N. Atkinson. It took part under Lawton, Gordon and Evans in all the battles in Virginia, Maryland and Pennsylvania, from June, 1862. to April, 1865, at Appomattox, when it surrendered with less than one hundred men.

No better Regiment ever fought for the South.

Flag of the **Thirty-fifth Georgia Regiment.** Commanded by Colonel (afterwards General) Ed. L. Thomas, and formed part of Thomas' Brigade, A. P. Hill's Third Corps.

Served under Jackson until his death, when the Third Corps was organized and placed under command of General A. P. Hill.

Took part in all the battles and campaigns in Virginia, Maryland and Pennsylvania, and surrendered at Appomattox.

Flag of the **Forty-fourth Georgia Regiment.** Commanded by the gallant Robert A. Smith of Macon, Ga., and was one of the Regiments of J. G. Walker's, then R. S. Ripley's Brigade, D. H. Hill's Division, Army of Northern Virginia.

After General Ripley had been severely wounded, Gen. Geo. Doles became the Brigade Commander, and the Forty-fourth Regiment remained in this Brigade until its surrender.

On May 10 1864, at Spottsylvania C. H., General Upton's storming column of ten picked Regiments assaulted Doles's Brigade of four small Regiments and captured about 60 per cent of this Regiment, among them the Color Bearer. For twenty minutes Upton's men held a small part of the Confederate line, but Gordon's Brigade came to the assistance

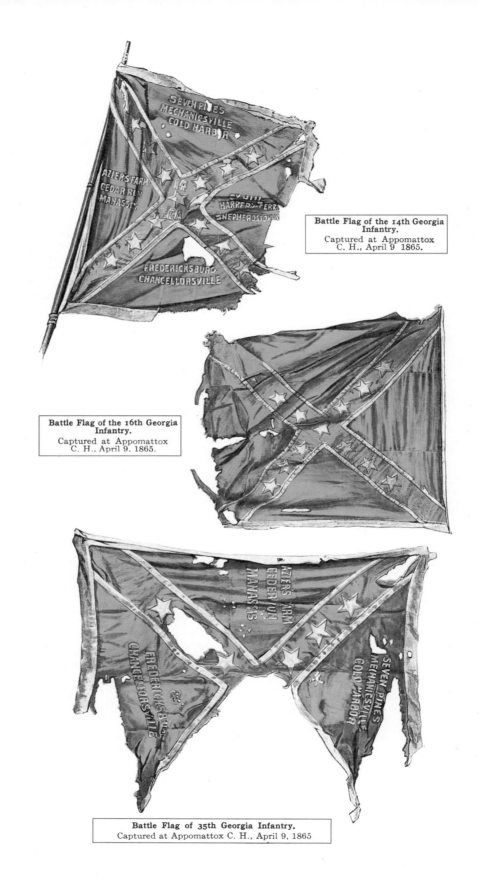

Battle Flag of the 14th Georgia
Infantry.
Captured at Appomattox
C. H., April 9 1865.

Battle Flag of the 16th Georgia
Infantry.
Captured at Appomattox
C. H., April 9. 1865.

Battle Flag of 35th Georgia Infantry.
Captured at Appomattox C. H., April 9, 1865

of Doles and the Federals were driven back. The Forty-fourth served during the war and surrendered at Appomattox.

Flag of the **Forty-fifth Georgia Regiment.** The Forty-fifth Georgia Regiment, Colonels Thos. Hardeman, Jr. and Thomas J. Simmons, was one of the Regiments of Thomas's Brigade, Pender's Division, A. P. Hill's Corps. It fought wherever the Army of Northern Virginia fought, and was a most gallant command. They surrendered at Appomattox C. H. Col. Simmons is now the honored Chief Justice of the Supreme Court of Georgia.

Flag of the **Forty-ninth Georgia Regiment.** This Regiment was also one of General E. L. Thomas's Georgia Brigade of Pender's Division, A. P. Hill's Third Corps, Army of Northern Virginia. It participated gallantly in all the campaigns in Virginia, Maryland and Pennsylvania, and surrendered at Appomattox C. H., April 9, 1865. The rank and file were from among the sturdy, full-blooded Middle Georgia Americans, many of them men of wealth, and all of them patriotic.

Flag of the **Fiftieth Georgia Regiment.** The Fiftieth Regiment was from the Southern Counties of Georgia, and was one of the Regiments of General Paul J. Semmes's Brigade, McLaw's Division, Longstreet's Corps, Army of Northern Virginia.

It was commanded by Colonel W. R. Manning and Peter McGlashern, the latter now commanding the Georgia Division of United Confederate Veterans.

This Regiment participated in all the battles in which the Army of Northern Virginia was engaged and surrendered at Appomattox.

Flag of the **Fifty-first Georgia Regiment.** This Regiment was one of General Paul J. Semmes's Brigade, and served in the Army of Northern Virginia. It belonged to McLaw's Division, Longstreet's Corps, participated in the battles in Virginia, Maryland and Pennsylvania, and surrendered at Appomattox.

It was a fine command and reflected honor upon Georgia on many a hard-fought field.

Flag of the **Sixtieth Georgia Regiment.** This was one of the Regiments of the Georgia Brigade first commanded by General A. R. Lawton, one of Georgia's distinguished soldiers and citizens, who becoming disabled for field service by wounds, was appointed Quartermaster-General by President Davis.

General Gordon succeeded him, and after his promotion, General Clement A. Evans subsequently commanded the Division to the close of the battle of Appomattox, and is now Commander of the Army of Tennessee Department, U. C. V.

This Regiment took part in all the battles in Virginia, Maryland and Pennsylvania, and surrendered at Appomattox; taking part in the last battle, joining in the last successful charge of Jackson's Old Division, commanded by General Evans, even after the flag of truce had been sent in.

Notice of the truce and surrender was carried from Gordon to Evans by one of General Sheridan's Staff Officers, or Couriers.

Flag of the **Sumter Flying Artillery.** This Company was from Americus, Sumter County, Ga., and was commanded by Captain Allen S. Cutts, who was afterwards promoted Lieutenant-Colonel, and given command of the Eleventh Battalion of Artillery, more familiarly known as Cutts' Battalion.

This flag was surrendered at Sailor's Creek, near Appomattox, four days before General Lee surrendered the Army of Northern Virginia.

The Sumter Flying Artillery did great service in all the campaigns of the Army of Northern Virginia, and was one of the best Artillery Companies furnished by Georgia.

Flag of **Cobb's Legion of Infantry.** This Regiment was one of Cobb's Georgia Brigade, commanded by Col. Thos. R. R. Cobb, who was afterwards promoted to Brigadier-General.

It was in all the engagements fought by the Army of Northern Virginia.

At Fredericksburg, December 13, 1862, this Brigade held the advance line in front of Mayre's Hill, and repulsed repeated assaults by Burnside's right wing. They were aided late in the fight by Kershaw's and Ransom's Brigades, but refused to leave the post of honor. Gen. Thos. Cobb was killed in this battle, and Gen. W. T. Wofford afterwards commanded it.

At Crampton's Gap, Maryland, in September, 1862, this Regiment was overwhelmed by parts of Franklin's Corps of McClellan's Army. Lieut.-Col. Jeff Lamar was mortally wounded while commanding. He had received one wound, and was lying on the field. Near by were other wounded men, among them Lieut. Wm. B. Lowe. Lieut. Lowe said that the command was being surrounded and called to Col. Lamar to order his regiment out of the perilous position it was vainly trying to hold. This heroic officer asked the Lieutenant to hold him up until he could give the command. The wounded Lieutenant crawled to his side, and with painful effort raised his Colonel to his feet. With superhuman effort he ordered his regiment to move, **"By the left flank, double quick."** Just as he issued the order another vengeful bullet passed through his body and the Lieutenant gently laid him down to die among his heroic comrades.

With such officers, Cobb's Legion could not have been anything except a glorious command.

W. H. Harrison,
Adjutant, Atlanta Camp No. 159, U. C. V., Atlanta, Ga.

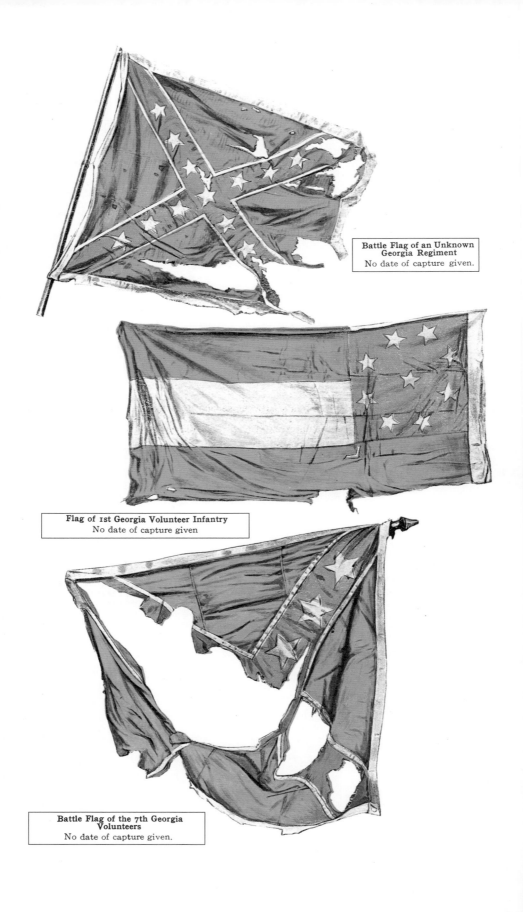

Battle Flag of an Unknown
Georgia Regiment
No date of capture given.

Flag of 1st Georgia Volunteer Infantry
No date of capture given

Battle Flag of the 7th Georgia
Volunteers
No date of capture given.

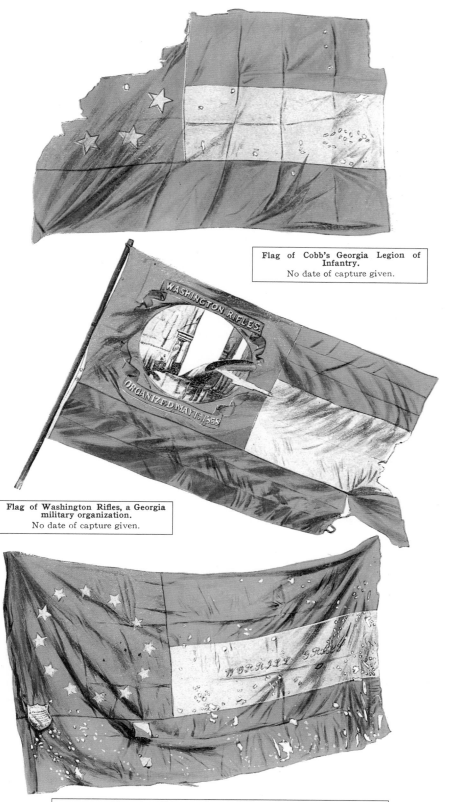

Flag of Cobb's Georgia Legion of Infantry.
No date of capture given.

Flag of Washington Rifles, a Georgia military organization.
No date of capture given.

Flag of an Unknown Georgia Military Organization.
No date of capture given.

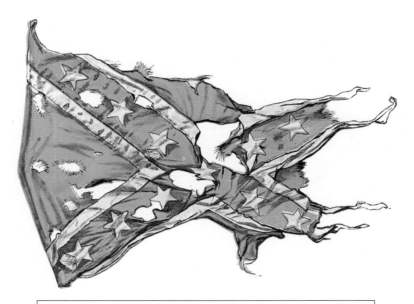

Flag of the 10th Missouri Battery (Barrett's).
Captured at Columbus, Ga., April 16, 1865.

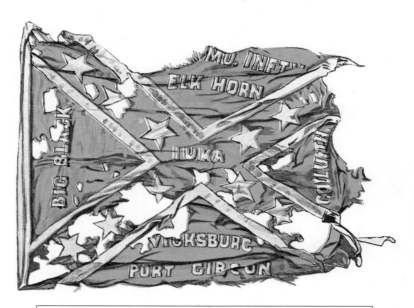

Flag of an Unknown Missouri Infantry Regiment.
Captured at the Battle of Franklin, November 30, 1864.

Missouri Confederate Flags.

We have been unable to secure any information in regard to the Confederate flags of Missouri excepting the information contained in the letter below from the Adjutant General of the State of Missouri:

MAY 24th, 1905.

Mr. Charles E. Ware,
    Manager Buxton & Skinner Stationery Co.,
      St. Louis, Missouri.

Dear Sir:—

The flags recently returned to the State of Missouri by the War Department, and of which photographs were sent you by Mr. Simms of this City, are two in number.

The first is of the **Tenth Missouri Battery,** otherwise known as **Barrett's Battery.** The flag was captured with its bearer at Columbus, Ga., April 16, 1865, by Private John Kenney of the Fourth Iowa Cavalry, after a struggle with its bearer for possession of the flag.

The other, larger, flag is that of a **Missouri Infantry Regiment.** The number of the Regiment has been torn off, and I am unable to give it. The names of six battles, in which the flag was carried, have been sewed on the flag. They are "Big Black," "Elk Horn," "Iuka," "Corinth," "Vicksburg," "Port Gibson," also another beginning "Kers—," with the last letters missing. Upon the flag is printed in ink, "Captured by Sergt. Alfred . . . . . . (last name blurred) Company K, Ninety-seventh O. V. I., at the Battle of Franklin, November 30, 1864."

I regret that I am not able to give you further information. There are in this Office no Confederate Records, and none of the Confederate Veterans who have looked at these flags have been able to give me any further part of their history.

I am, very respectfully,

James A. DeArmond.
Adjutant General.

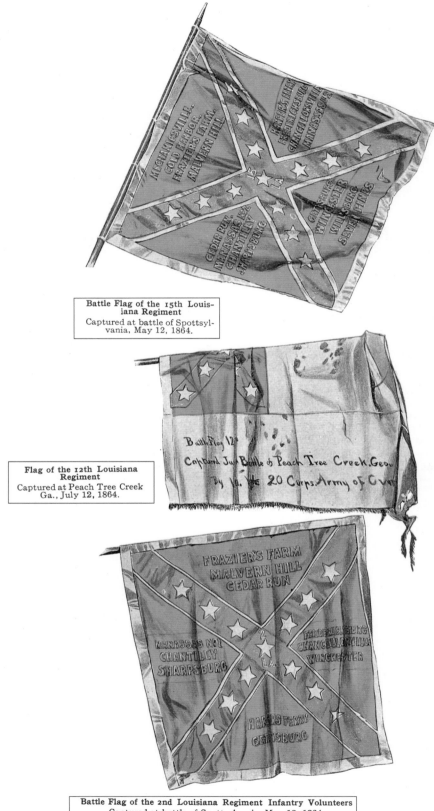

Battle Flag of the 15th Louisiana Regiment
Captured at battle of Spottsylvania, May 12, 1864.

Flag of the 12th Louisiana
Regiment
Captured at Peach Tree Creek
Ga., July 12, 1864.

Battle Flag of the 2nd Louisiana Regiment Infantry Volunteers
Captured at battle of Spottsylvania, May 12, 1864.

Flag of Austin's Battalion, Louisiana.
Captured at Columbus, Ga., April 16, 1865.

Louisiana.

CAPTURED BATTLE FLAGS OF THE CONFEDERACY.

Returned to Louisiana Division, U. C. V.

The presentation of returned Confederate Flags which occurred in New Orleans, April 13th, in Memorial Hall, was an event freighted with significance, and tinged with tenderest sentiment.

The occasion was an auspicious one, being as it were an open avowal and assurance of the healing of all old wounds, forcibly indicative of the golden epoch of amicable relationship between the north and south.

Faded, blood-stained and bullet-rent these revered relics were unfurled to view, and, as they fluttered once again over the assemblage of Confederate veterans, associations were potent in recalling an era hallowed within the memory of every loyal-hearted southerner.

Like receiving an old comrade back into the ranks, these emblems of a loved lost cause were welcomed with reverent ovation by the old soldiers who fought so valiantly under their glowing standards.

With uncovered head, softened tread and whispered breath, one pauses before the case of treasured mementoes, and, gazing upon their tattered remnants bearing time-faded inscriptions, is inspired with a feeling of sacred reverence for the silent story of heroism, bloodshed and sacrifice they reveal—while the following beautiful lines are brought to mind:

"Not long unfurled was I known,
      For Fate was against me;
  But I flashed over a Pure Cause
      And on land and sea
  So fired the hearts of men into heroism
      That the world honored me.
  Within my folds the dead who died under me
      Lie fitly shrouded,
  And my tattered colors,
      Crowded with a thousand shining victories,
  Have become for the people who love me,
      A glorified memory."

Flag of the **Second Louisiana Regiment Infantry Volunteers.** This flag of regulation infantry battle flag, four feet square with two-inch yellow binding ornamented with white silk stars and half-inch wide silk fillet, bears the numbers 192 in black stenciled figures and between the bands of the cross on its red field are inscribed the following battles: Frazier's Farm, Malvern Hill, Cedar Run, Manassas No. 2, Chantilly, Sharpsburg, Fredericksburg, Chancellorsville, Winchester No. 2, Harper's Ferry, Gettysburg.

The flag of this regiment bears many bullet scars and tatters, showing the active service it has been through. This flag is very likely the one for the capture of which a medal of Honor was awarded, as the following extract from the list of such records as are to be found concerning it:

"Charles H. Fasnacht, Sergeant Company A, Ninety-ninth Pennsylvania Infantry, May 12, 1864, captured flag of Second Louisiana Tigers, at Spottsylvania, Va."

Flag of the **Second Louisiana Regiment Infantry.** This flag of regulation infantry design is made of bunting with white binding forming a border, white silk stars and white silk fillet half-inch wide forms an ornamentation around the blue cross. It leaves the number 180 in stenciled black figures on the white binding.

This flag is reported to have seen little battle service at the time of its capture, in consequence of which there are no bullet rents marring its wholeness and no battles inscribed. The only thing defacing its surface is a few moth-eaten spots. It is attached to a short, rough-hewn staff. Accompanying this flag is the following legend, which appears to have been written some days after its capture, and signed by Brig.-Gen. G. W. Getty: "The flag of the Second Louisiana regiment was captured in the battle of the 22d of September, 1864, at Fisher's Hill near Strasburg, Va., by Private James Connor, Company F, Forty-Third New York Volunteers Sharp Shooters, at Headquarters, Second Division, Sixth Corps, in the earthworks occupied by Carpenter's Rebel Battery. Signed, G. W. Getty, Harrisonburg, Va., Brigadier-General, commanding. In this battle the Second Louisiana was attached to Staffeed's Brigade of Maj.-Gen. John B. Geedon's Division.

This brigade seems to have held its part of the works at Fisher's Hill until most others had left, when the Federals flanked the left of the Confederate line, which crumbled to pieces from left to right.

Eighth Louisiana Regiment Infantry Battle Flag. The legend attached to this standard shows that its capture was effected November 7, 1863, at Rappahannock Station, Va., by Lieut. A. S. Lyon, Company K, Fifth Maine Volunteers.

The flag is attached to a light staff, seven feet high that has been broken and the breaks secured by a tin tube. Accompanying this flag was a wooden spear-head with battle ax cross piece painted black, which must have surmounted the staff and was broken off.

Flag of the **Twelfth Louisiana.** This flag returned as having been captured from the Twelfth Louisiana Regiment Infantry, is a large national Confederate flag, 88 inches long by 50 inches wide. It is made of close-woven bunting, with a yellow fringe around it. It is the second pattern Confederate flag, white field with white fillet along the blue cross. Painted in black on the white field is the following legend: "Twelfth Louisiana, One Hundred and Fifth Regiment, Illinois Infantry, Twentieth Volunteer Corps, of the Cumberland." This flag shows that it has been through active service by reason of the bullet rents and blood stains upon it. It is also very badly moth eaten.

The Twelfth Louisiana Regiment in this battle was part of Brig.-Gen. T. M. Scott's Brigade of Loring's Division of Stewart's Corps, Col. Noel L. Nelson was in command of the regiment. In a charge of its brigade on the 12th of July in what is called the battle of Peach Tree Creek, in front of Atlanta, the brigade was repulsed, and the Twelfth Louisiana suffered heavily owing to the failure of an adjoining command to advance in line.

In Col. Nelson's report of this battle he mentioned no loss of colors, but states out of 318 men the regiment had 57 killed and wounded, and 9 missing. The loss had fallen mainly on three companies of the regiment, that pushed farthest forward in the charge.

In the same records is to be found the report of Lieut.-Col. E. F. Dutton, commanding the One Hundred and Fifth Illinois Volunteers. "Among the trophies captured by my command was one set of colors claimed by Rebel wounded to belong to the Twelfth Louisiana Infantry." This is the flag described above.

Flag (so called) of **Thirteenth Louisiana Regiment**—Really the **Fifteenth Louisiana Regiment.** This flag was sent and on the legends attached to it is designated as that of the Thirteenth Louisiana Regiment. This was evidently not properly examined at the time of its capture or when the legends were placed upon it. On the yellow figures one and one-half inches high it bears the number 15 and the letters La., proving it to be the flag of the Fifteenth Louisiana Regiment Infantry . The battles inscribed on it were all fought by the army of Northern Virginia to which the Fifteenth Louisiana was attached. The Thirteenth Louisiana Regiment Infantry was attached to the Army of Tennessee C. S. A. and never fought in the field of operations of the Army of Northern Virginia.

The flag described was captured by Philip Schlaterer, Private, Company F, Seventy-third New York Infantry, May 12, 1864, at Spottsylvania, Va. The flag is of bunting of

Battle Flag of Bouanchaud's Battery, Pointe Coupee Artillery
Captured at Battle of Nashville, Dec. 16, 1864.

regulation battle flag size for infantry. It is four feet square, with two inches white bunting binding, white silk stars and three-quarter of an inch fillet along the blue cross. On the outside white binding it bears the number 133, in one and one-half inch stenciled black figures, and the same in ink on the cloth legend. In yellow paint stands the number 15 above the center star and La. below it in one and one-half inch figures. The following battles are inscribed upon this flag: Cold Harbor, Malvern Hill, Cedar Run, Manassas No. 2, Chantilly, Sharpsburg, Harper's Ferry, Fredericksburg, Charlottesville, Manassas No. 1, Gettysburg, Winchester, Williamsburg, Seven Pines. The flag is rent and torn in many places by bullets and shell, but otherwise is in a good state of preservation.

The flag was captured at the same time as that of the Second Louisiana Regiment, when Hancock, the Federal General, carried the bloody angle and broke through the Confederate lines where stood Col. Johnson's division, on the 12th of May, 1864, at Spottsylvania.

Flag of the **Twenty-fourth Louisiana Regiment.** The legend inscribed in ink along the white fillet that bordered the blue cross upon this standard is as follows:

"Twenty-fourth Infantry Battle Flag, captured by First-Lieut. W. S. Simmons, Company Eleventh Missouri Volunteers at battle of Brentwood Hills near Nashville, December 16, 1864."

Lieut. Simmons was awarded a medal of Honor for this capture. Two other flags were captured at the same time by the Eleventh Missouri, but in both cases it is stated that no definite idea exists as to the regiment they belonged.

The Louisiana Infantry commands in that battle were the First, Fourth, Thirteenth, Sixteenth, Twentieth, Twenty-fifth, Thirtieth Regiments, and Fourteenth Battalion composing Gen. R. L. Gibson's Brigade of Gen. H. D. Clayton's Division, Stephen D. Lee's

Corps. This division was the right of the corps. It repulsed the attacks of the enemy and left its works only after the whole line to the left had been broken.

The flag is after the battle flag pattern for Infantry, being 5 feet square, made of loose woven bunting with white stars, border and fillet of cotton cloth. The fillet is an inch wide and bears the number 211 in black stenciled figures, one and one-half-inch high. It is marked with blood and torn by bullets and shell; appearing by these defacements to have seen much active service.

Flag of **Austin's Battalion.** This flag belonged to Austin's Battalion and was captured at Columbus, Ga., April 16, 1865, with its bearer a sergeant, by private Andrew Tibbett, Third Iowa Cavalry, First Brigade, Fourth Division, Cavalry Corps, M D. M., inside the line of works and to the right of the four gun battery on the right of the enemy's line. The flag is of the Confederate national pattern, white fillet with battle flag of the union in upper corner. It is of fine material and beautifully made. This flag was made by the ladies of Mobile and sent to the Battalion at the opening of the war. Inscribed on it in red letters two inches high are the names, Austin's Battalion, Shiloh, Belmont, Chickamauga, Farmington, Murfreesboro, and bears crossed cannons also in red cloth six inches long below the battle flag union. The stars of the battle flag are of white silk and the fillet along the blue cross of the same material. Andrew W. Tibbett received a medal of Honor for the capture of this flag.

Flag of **Bouanchaud's Battery Pointe Coupee Artillery.** The following legend is inscribed on the red field of this flag, captured from Bouanchaud's Battery at the battle of Nashville, December 16, 1864.

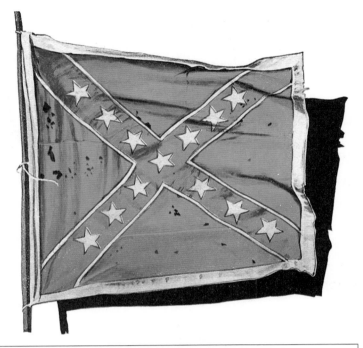

Battle Flag of 2nd Louisiana Regiment Infantry
Captured in Battle of Fisher's Hill, Sept. 22, 1864.

"Bouanchaud's Battery Flag. Captured by William May, Private, Company H, Thirty-third Iowa Infantry, Second Brigade, Second Division Detachment, Army of Tennessee, at the battle of Brentwood Hills, near Nashville, December 16, 1864."

Report of Col. William R. Marshall, Seventh Minnesota Infantry, commanding Third Brigade, First Division Detachment, Army of Tennessee, says: "Most bravely did the lines rise with cheers, breasting the storm of shot and shell from four guns in our front, charge and carry the strong works on the left of the Cranny White Pike. The splendid Pointe Coupee Battery of four Napoleon twelve pounders, a great number of small arms and 300 to 400 prisoners were taken.

"William May, a private of Capt. Benson's Company H, Thirty-second Iowa, as the Company approached the works, dashed forward and captured the battery and guidon. Several official papers of this battery were also captured, proving it to have been A. Bouanchaud's."

William May's interesting account of the incidentals told as follows: "On the 16th of December when the Second Brigade, Second Division, Detachment Army of Tennessee, was ordered to charge the enemy's works as, my regiment, the Thirty-second Iowa Infantry, was on the right of the Brigade approached the earthworks, I saw this rebel battery flag with the guns, and ran ahead of the regiment over the works, and took it out of the Rebel's hand. In a valise close by, I found some brass buttons, manufactured at Montgomery with letter B., German text. Also a captain's shoulder straps, some papers, invoices of ordinance stores, etc., showing the Battery to have been A. Bouanchaud's'." The flag is about four feet square of crimson bunting with yellow fringe, bearing a diagonal cross, upon which are thirteen silken stars. The flag shows little of the wear and tear of active service, and must have been found in Capt. Bouanchaud's valise, which it is claimed, the captor must have thoroughly explored.

Flag of the **Washington Artillery.** This flag, concerning the capture of which a confliction of opinion has ever existed, is one of the most interesting of the group of tattered emblems.

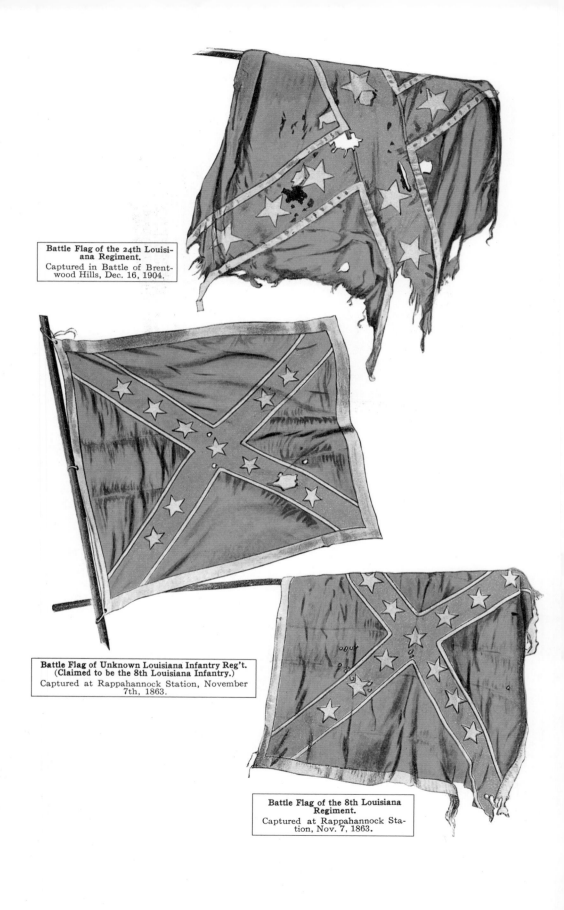

Battle Flag of the 24th Louisiana Regiment.
Captured in Battle of Brentwood Hills, Dec. 16, 1904.

Battle Flag of Unknown Louisiana Infantry Reg't.
(Claimed to be the 8th Louisiana Infantry.)
Captured at Rappahannock Station, November
7th, 1863.

Battle Flag of the 8th Louisiana
Regiment.
Captured at Rappahannock Sta-
tion, Nov. 7, 1863.

Many doubts were expressed as to the authentic capture of this flag. When, however, it was first removed from the case upon the night of the presentation, and after careful unrolling and examination all doubts were banished, for it proved to be the veritable standard of the Second Company of this Battalion. When straightened out, the binding revealed the inscription: **"Second Company Washington Artillery of N. O."** Colonel John B. Richardson, who commanded this company at Appomattox, testified to the identity of this returned flag as being the battle flag of his Company, and the writing upon it, as that of Sergeant Caesar Huchez, one of its members. The flag is of close woven bunting, three feet square, of regulation artillery-battery pattern, bordered with a two-inch white cotton binding, while white silken stars and fillets adorn the edges of the blue cross. It is numbered 303, in one and one-half-inch figures, stenciled in black on the red field. The name of the Company is inscribed upon the upper border in large letters. The upper border is separated from the main body of the flag by a rent extending its full length.

This glorious standard of one of Louisiana's most valiant regiments shows the ravages of battle. Tattered, torn and streaked with blood, which in many places obliterate the bright, little white silk stars, while the black spots here and there show the passage through and along it of bullets and shells.

This flag is still attached to the staff that bore it in its last battle.

Of this flag, Col. Richardson says, that during that last battle of April 8th at Appomattox Station, he handed the flag into the keeping of Private William W. Davis, a splendid soldier, with instructions to secrete it on his person. Nothing was ever heard of this noble young hero after the trust imposed upon him by his superior officer.

It was nightfall when the fighting began with the Federal Cavalry, that had cut through the column of the retiring Artillery, and the battle raged unceasingly throughout the night. The flag was evidently captured from Davis before he could carry out his commanding officer's instructions, and the blood which stains this flag must be that shed by the gallant soldier in his struggle to preserve it from the enemy.

This flag was captured in the Battle of Appomattox Station, April 8, 1865, by Barney Shields, Company E, Second Virginia Volunteers Cavalry, Third Brigade. Cavalry Division, Brevet Major-General George A. Custer, commanding.

Rebellion records show the following list of medals of Honor awarded is to be found: "Bernard Shields, Private Company E, Second West Virginia Cavalry, April 8, 1865, captured flag of the Washington Artillery at Appomattox, Va."

Flag of an **Unknown or Uncertain Louisiana Infantry Regiment.** This flag is the regulation infantry battle flag of bunting, four feet square, white binding two inches around the flag, while the blue cross is ornamented with white silken stars and white fillet half-inch wide. It has several patches and its flying end is ravelled and torn; it shows bullet marks and is slightly moth eaten.

The number 14 is marked on the white cotton cloth sewed in one corner, on which is written the following legend:

"Confederate battle flag of the **Eighth Louisiana Regiment,** captured at Rappahannock Station, Va., November 7, 1863, by Sergeant Otis C. Roberts, Sixth Regiment, Maine Volunteers, Sixth Brigade, First Division, Sixth Army Corps, captured in hand to hand fight in trenches."

There are no battles inscribed on it, nor any number or letters designating it as belonging to the Eighth Louisiana Regiment.

This Regiment belonged to Brig.-Gen. Harry T. Hays' Brigade, which on November 7, 1863, at Rappahannock Station, was mostly all captured by the Federal Gen. Sedgwick's Corps. Gen. Meade reports having there taken four Colonels, three Lieutenant-Colonels, many other officers and 800 men prisoners, together with the capture of four battle flags.

The account of the capture of this flag is as follows:

"Sergeant Otis O. Roberts, of Company H, with only five men rushed upon the color bearer of the Eighth Louisiana Regiment who was in the midst of his color company, and after a hand to hand fight, in which bayonets were freely used, succeeded in capturing the colors and compelling the company to surrender. Sergeant Roberts was awarded a medal for his valiant deed of capture."

T. W. CASTLEMAN,
Adjutant-General and Chief of Staff,
Louisiana Division United Confederate Veterans,
New Orleans, La.

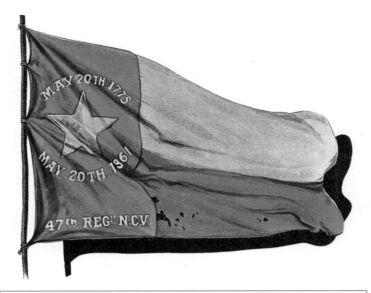

Flag Carried by the 47th Regiment, North Carolina Volunteers.
No date of capture given.

North Carolina Flags.

Owing to the fact that the returned Confederate flags of North Carolina have been carefully grouped in large cases in the Hall of History, at Raleigh, it was impossible, in the short time before which this publication had to be issued, to secure pictures of all of the flags in the collection so they could be reproduced separately. Below, however, is given the history complete of the flags returned by the Government to the State of North Carolina.

North Carolina bears the enviable record of having sent more troops to the Confederate service than any other state in the south and of having lost more men in battle.

The flags which were returned here late last March by the United States War Department to Governor Robert B. Glenn were placed in the charge of the director of the Hall of History, and were by him arranged in four cases made of native woods, being so displayed as to produce a very fine effect, to show the number of the Regiment and also the inscriptions covering the battles in which each Regiment participated. It is thought that in no other state has such an arrangement been carried out. There are thirty-two of the flags. Eleven of these are upon the staffs. Some of the staffs are mere poles, and in one case the staff is a pine stick, with the bark still on. In this case a letter has been received from the color-bearer in which he says that the flag was being taken to the rear by the regiment, which was retreating from an overwhelming force; that the flag caught in the thick undergrowth, but that he tore it away and left the staff, stopping further in the woods and cutting the little pine sapling. The flags show the great number of engagements in which the North Carolina troops participated. Most of them are from the Army of Northern Virginia, but one is from the Western Army, and this is specially displayed, being that of the Thirty-ninth Infantry. A monument is to be dedicated in July at Chickamauga to the North Carolinians who lost their lives in that great battle, in which eight regiments from this state participated.

There are also in the Hall of History a number of other Confederate flags of peculiar interest, notably among these being the "Bethel" flag, which is that which was borne by the

Battle Flag of the 38th North Carolina Regiment.
No date of capture given.

First Regiment of Volunteers at the battle of Bethel, Va., in June, 1861, where the regiment, constituting the principal force of the Confederates and under command of Colonel (afterwards Lieutenant-General) Daniel Harvey Hill, so distinguished itself in the defeat of the Federals that the North Carolina Legislature, then in session, directed that the name "Bethel" should be inscribed upon the flag, this name appearing in blue silk. The regiment was also given the distinctive name of the "Bethel Regiment" and hence had no number, even in the re-organization of the North Carolina troops.

Another flag was that used at the headquarters of Major-General Bryan Grimes, the ranking officer of the North Carolina troops at Appomattox, under whose direction the last charge was made at Appomattox Court House on early Monday morning, April 9, 1865, when the Confederate infantry, under command of General William R. Cox, fired the last volley and drove back the Federal line, and the cavalry made a capture of four guns of a Federal battery of regulars, of the Fourth Artillery, while the Confederate sharp-shooters, posted in a house, kept up so accurate a fire as to enable the Confederates to retire after having accomplished these two objects. The Grimes flag was displayed at his headquarters and was not taken down until after the surrender, when it was cut away from the staff and brought back to Raleigh by one of General Grimes' couriers, who wrapped it around his body, under all his clothing.

Another flag of marked interest is that of the **Twenty-sixth North Carolina Regiment,** which was in turn commanded by Z. B. Vance (afterwards Governor and U. S. Senator). Henry King Burgwyn and John R. Lane, the latter of whom is still living near Raleigh. Col. Burgwyn was killed at Gettysburg, where his regiment, as stated by Col. Fox in the latter's well-known book, "Regimental Losses in Battle," suffered a greater loss than any other regiment, on either side, during the entire Civil War.

These flags attract a great deal of attention, as do the hundreds of other war relics shown in the great collection, the latter being grouped according to periods, so as to show the history of the state from its earliest settlement in 1585 down to the present time. A complete list of the flags is appended, which the writer made after a personal inspection of every flag.

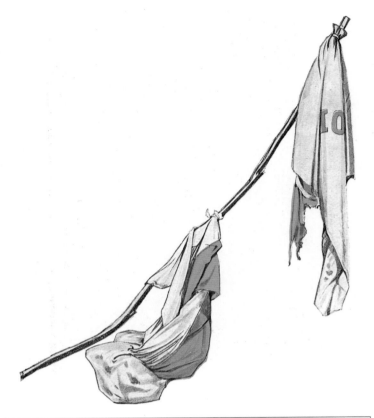

All the flags are what are known as battle flags, except four, the battle flags being square in shape, of solid red bunting, with cross-bars and with stars thereon of white. In almost every case the regiment is painted in yellow above the center star and with the letters "N. C." below the star. Unless mention is made otherwise, all the flags described are of the battle flag class. The following is the list:

First Regiment. Captured May 12, 1864, by Private D. W. Harris, Company B, One Hundred and Forty-eighth Pennsylvania Regiment, in the charge of the Second Army Corps on the morning of that day. The names of the following battles appear on the flag, being marked in stencil, in black letters: Winchester, No. 2, Gettysburg, Boonesboro, Sharpsburg, Fredericksburg, Chancellorsville, Mechanicsville, Cold Harbor, Malvern Hill.

Fourth Regiment. No inscription as to its fate. Names of battles: Seven days around Richmond, First and Second Fredericksburg, Chancellorsville, first and second Maryland campaigns, Spotsylvania, Valley campaign, Seven Pines.

Battle Flag, **Sixth North Carolina Regiment.** Captured at Rappahannock Station. Va., May 7, 1863, by James H. Littlefield, Company F, Fifth Maine Volunteers.

Sixth Regiment. Captured at Sailor's Creek, April 6, 1865, by Private James Kimball, Company B, Second Regiment West Virginia Cavalry. No inscription showing battles.

Seventh Regiment. Captured at Gettysburg, July 3, 1865, by Private John E. Mayberry. Company F, First Delaware Regiment. Names of battles: Newbern, Hanover, Mechanicsville, Cold Harbor, Frazier's Farm, Malvern Hill, Cedar Run, Manassas Junction, Manassas Plains, Ox Hill, Harper's Ferry, Sharpsburg, Shepherdstown, Fredericksburg, Wilderness, Chancellorsville.

Twelfth Regiment. No inscription as to how taken, and no names of battles, the flag being very badly mutilated.

Flag carried by the 46th Regiment North Carolina Volunteers
This flag has been all shot away excepting the red field shown.
No date of capture given.

Thirteenth Regiment. No statement as to fate. Names of battles: Cold Harbor, Malvern Hill, South Mountain, Sharpsburg, Fredericksburg, Chancellorsville.

Thirteenth Regiment. Captured May 6, 1864, by Sergeant S. Wrought, Company A, One Hundred and Forty-first Pennsylvania Regiment. Names of battles: Williamsburg, Seven Pines, Cold Harbor, Malvern Hill, South Mountain, Sharpsburg, Fredericksburg, Chancellorsville.

Sixteenth Regiment. Captured at Gettysburg, July 3, 1863, by fourteen Connecticut volunteers. Names of battles: Seven Pines, Mechanicsville, Cold Harbor, Frazier's Farm, Cedar Run, Manassas, Ox Hill, Harper's Ferry, Sharpsburg, Shepherdstown, Chancellorsville, Fredericksburg.

Eighteenth Regiment. Captured May 21, 1864, by Lieutenant A. H. Mitchell, One Hundred and Fifth Pennsylvania. Names of battles: Hanover, Mechanicsville, Cold Harbor, Frazier's Farm, Malvern Hill, Cedar Run, Manassas Junction, Manassas Plains, Ox Hill, Harper's Ferry, Sharpsburg, Shepherdstown, Fredericksburg, Wilderness, Chancellorsville.

Eighteenth Regiment. Captured at Malvern Hill, July 20, 1864, by Private Timothy Connors, Company E, First United States Cavalry. Names of battles: Hanover, Mechanicsville, Cold Harbor, Frazier's Farm, Cedar Run, Malvern Hill, Manassas Junction, Manassas Plains, Ox Hill, Harper's Ferry, Sharpsburg, Shepherdstown, Chancellorsville, Fredericksburg.

Eighteenth Regiment. Captured near Petersburg, April 2, 1865, by Private Frank Fesq, Company A, Fortieth New Jersey. Names of battles: Wilderness, Chancellorsville, Gettysburg, Falling Waters, Cedar Run, Manassas Junction, Manassas Plains, Ox Hill, Harper's Ferry, Shepherdstown, Fredericksburg, Sharpsburg, Hanover, Mechanicsville, Cold Harbor, Frazier's Farm, Malvern Hill.

Twenty-second Regiment. Captured by Private McDonough, Forty-second New York. Names of battles: Seven Pines, Mechanicsville, Cold Harbor, Frazier's Farm, Cedar Run, Manassas, Ox Hill, Harper's Ferry, Sharpsburg, Shepherdstown, Fredericksburg, Chancellorsville.

Twenty-third Regiment. Captured by Second Division, First Army Corps, at Gettysburg, July 2, 1863. Names of battles: Seven Pines, Malvern Hill, South Mountain, Mechanicsville, Cold Harbor, Sharpsburg, Fredericksburg.

Twenty-fourth Regiment. Captured August 21, 1864, by Private J. A. Reed, Eleventh Pennsylvania. No names of battles.

Twenty-fourth Regiment. Captured by Private David Edwards, One Hundred and Forty-sixth New York Volunteers, April 1, 1865, in battle. No names of battles.

Twenty-sixth. Captured by Sergeant Alonzo Smith, Seventh Michigan, at Hatcher's Run, October 27, 1864. No names of battles.

Twenty-eighth Regiment. Captured by Corporal J. M. Condig, Company A, Sixty-third Pennsylvania, May 12, 1864. Names of battles: Hanover, Mechanicsville, Cold Harbor, Frazier's Farm, Malvern Hill, Cedar Run, Manassas Junction, Manassas Plains, Ox Hill, Harper's Ferry, Sharpsburg, Shepherdstown, Fredericksburg, Wilderness, Chancellorsville.

Twenty-eighth Regiment. No statement as to fate. Names of battles: Hanover, Mechanicsville, Cold Harbor, Frazier's Farm, Malvern Hill, Cedar Run, Manassas Junction, Manassas Plains, Ox Hill, Harper's Ferry, Shepherdstown, Fredericksburg, Sharpsburg, Wilderness, Chancellorsville, Gettysburg, Falling Waters.

Thirtieth Regiment. No statement as to fate. Names of battles: Seven days around Richmond, first and second Fredericksburg, Chancellorsville, first and second Maryland campaigns.

Thirtieth Regiment. No statement as to fate. Names of battles: Seven days around Richmond, first and second Fredericksburg, Chancellorsville, first and second Maryland campaign. (Right side of flag damaged, part being apparently cut away, also part of lower right section of cross removed. One inscription which was painted on a slip of cloth sewed to the flag has faded, and is illegible.)

Thirtieth Regiment. Captured May 12, 1864, at the Wilderness. Names of battles: Mechanicsville, Cold Harbor, Malvern Hill, Boonesboro, Sharpsburg, Fredericksburg.

Thirty-third Regiment. Captured by First Sergeant J. Kemp, Company A, Fifth Michigan, May 6, 1864. Names of battles: Newbern, Hanover, Mechanicsville, Cold Harbor, Manassas Plains, Ox Hill, Harper's Ferry, Sharpsburg, Frazier's Farm, Malvern Hill, Cedar Run, Manassas Junction, Shepherdstown, Fredericksburg, Wilderness, Chancellorsville.

Thirty-fourth Regiment. No statement as to fate. Names of battles: Mechanicsville, Cold Harbor, Frazier's Farm, Cedar Run, Manassas, Ox Hill, Harper's Ferry, Sharpsburg, Shepherdstown, Fredericksburg, Chancellorsville.

Thirty-fourth Regiment. No statement as to fate. No names of battles. Thirteen stars of white in a blue field. Red, white and red bars.

Thirty-eighth Regiment. No statement as to fate. Names of battles: Cedar Run, Manassas, Ox Hill, Cold Harbor, Frazier's Farm, Harper's Ferry, Sharpsburg, Shepherdstown, Fredericksburg, Chancellorsville.

Thirty-ninth Regiment. No statement as to fate. Names of battles: Murfreesboro, Jackson, Chickamauga. These names are cut from white cloth and sewed on. The border of the flag next to the staff is of home-made canvas. The name of the regiment is given rather oddly, as the Thirty-ninth, "N. C. I.," the usual designation of regiments being "N. C. T."

Forty-fifth Regiment. Captured by Fifty-sixth Pennsylvania Volunteers, August 17, 1864, in battle near Globe Farm, on the Weldon Railway, near Petersburg. No names of battles.

Forty-sixth Regiment. No statement as to fate. No names of battles. This is merely the field of a State flag, the remainder having in some way been destroyed. The inscription is: "May 20, 1775, May 20, 1861," with a large white star between the inscriptions, and below them the words: Forty-sixth Regiment, N. C. V. The staff of this flag is shown. To it the flag was tied by a piece of shoe string and two pieces of twine.

Forty-seventh Regiment. No statement as to fate. No names of battles. This is also a State flag. The inscription is: "May 20, 1775; May 20, 1861." On a red field with a white star between the inscriptions the remainder of the flag being a blue bar and a white one. On the lower part appears: "Forty-seventh Regiment, N. C. V."

Forty-seventh Regiment. Captured by Sergeant Daniel Murphey, Nineteenth Massachusetts Regiment, at the battle of Hatcher's Run, October 2, 1864. No names of battles.

Fifty-second Regiment. Captured at Gettysburg, July 3, 1863. No names of battles.

Battle Flag, **Fifty-Fourth North Carolina Regiment,** on part of staff roughly made of wood, this flag being unique in having only twelve stars instead of the official thirteen. The War Department sends no statement as to the fate of this flag, but written with ink upon the fold of the flag around the staff are these words: "J. C. Gaunt, Company G., 104 O. V. I."

Col. F. A. Olds,
Director of the Hall of History, Raleigh, N. C.

Record of Rebel Flags Captured by Union Troops After April 19, 1861

1.   Confederate Flag Stars & Bars of 12th Virginia Volunteers, captured in Cavalry engagement near Beverly Ford, June 1863 by General Kilpatrick U. States Ord. Office *Returned 3/25/05.* 1

2.   Confederate Battle Flag of 5th Alabama Regiment, captured at Chancellorsville, Virginia, May 3rd 1863 by 111th Pennsylvania Volunteers, 3rd Brigade, 2nd Division 12th Corps *See 222* 2

3.   *18 Mississippi* Confederate Battle Flag captured May 3rd 1863 at Chancellorsville Virginia, by 77th New York Volunteers.   Brig. General A. P. Thomas' Division U. St. captured by Corpl Michael L James Co. F. Captor since killed. *Returned 3/25/05* W.W. 3

4.   Confederate Battle Flag of 10th Virginia Volunteers captured at Chancellorsville, Virginia, May 3rd 1863 by 68th Pennsylvania Volunteers *Returned 3/25/05.* 4

5.   Confederate Battle Flag captured at Sharpsburg, Maryland September 17th 1862 by 61st New York Volunteers, Caldwell's Brigade, Richardson's Division, Sumner's Corps Delivered to 61st N.Y. Vols. Dec 30th 1863 by order of Sect. of War *Returned to Ala 4/26/15* W. W.

6.   *54 N.C.* Confederate Battle Flag captured November 7th 1863 at Rappahannock Station, Virginia, by Corporal Theodore Shackelford Company "A" 5th Maine Volunteers Returned 4/25/05.

7.   Confederate Battle Flag captured at Rappahannock Station on November 7th 1863 by Philip Smith Co. E 121st New York Volunteers. *June 26th 1865 loaned to Col. E. Olcott 121 NY by order of the Secty of War.*

8.   Confederate Flag Stars & Bars "Citizen Soldiers The Best Defenders of our homes" W. W. Ord. Office 6

9.   Confederate Flag Stars & Bars Ord office. W.W. 7

10.   Confederate Flag of 1861 C. Ord. Office 8

11.   *8 La.* Confederate Battle Flag captured November 7, 1863 at the battle of Rappahannock Station Virginia, by Lieut. S. Lyons Co. K. 5th Maine Volunteers *Returned to LA 4/26/05* W.W.   Ord. office 9

12.   *6 N.C.* <u>Confederate Battle Flag</u> Captured at the Battle of Rappahannock Station, Virginia, November 7th 1863 by <u>James H. Littlefield</u> Co. I 5th Regiment Maine Volunteers. *Returned 4/26/05 to N.C. C. 10*

13.   <u>Confederate Battle Flag</u> captured at the battle of Sharpsburg, Maryland September 17th 1862 by Sedgwick's Division Sumner's Corps. W.W. Ord office. *11*

14.   <u>Confederate Battle Flag</u> of the 8th Louisiana Regiment captured at Rappahannock Station, Virginia, November 7th 1863 by Sergeant <u>Otis C. Roberts</u> 6th Regiment Maine Volunteers 3rd Brigade 1st Division 6th Army Corps. captured in a hand to hand fight on the trenches. *Returned 3/25/05 C 12*

15.   <u>Confederate Battle Flag</u> of the 1st Tennessee Battalion captured at Chickahomany June 27th 1862 by Seg't <u>John Marke</u> Company D 13th New York Volunteers, Martindale's Brigade, Morrell's Division. *Returned 4/26/05 W.W. Ord. office 13*

16.   <u>Confederate Flag</u> of "Yalusha Rifles" captured at Battle of Mills Springs, Ky, January 19, 1862 by Corporal <u>Albert Esson</u> Co. G 2nd Minnesota Volunteers *Returned 3/25/05 W.W. 14*

17.   *Va.* <u>Confederate Battle Flag</u> captured at Hanover, Pennsylvania July 1863, by Brig. General <u>Kilpatrick</u> forwarded Major General Sykes 5th Army Corps. *Returned to VA., 4/26/05 W.W. 15*

18.   <u>Confederate Battle Flag</u> captured at Chancellorsville, Virginia May 3rd 1863 by the 7th Ohio Regiment. C. *16*

19.   <u>Confederate Battle Flag</u> of 12th Georgia Volunteers captured at Chancellorsville, Virginia May 3rd, 1863 by 102nd New York Volunteers 3rd Brigade, 2nd Division, 12th Army Corps. *Returned 3/25/05 E.W.B. 17*

20.   <u>United States Flag</u> Stars & Stripes, captured at Battle of New Market Road, June 30th 1862, by <u>Patrick Ryan</u>, Co. D., 4th Regiment Pennsylvania Reserve Volunteer Corps, from the 11th Alabama Regiment. This flag was used by the Rebels to deceive the United States troops. Supposed to have been loaned and never returned.

21.   <u>Confederate Battle Flag</u> of 30th Alabama Regiment captured at Murfreesboro February 1863 by General A. G. McCook. *Returned 3/25/05 C. Ord. office. 18*

22.   Confederate Flag, Stars & Bars, captured at the Battle of Gettysburg Pennsylvania, July 2nd, 1863 by 60th Regiment New York Volunteers, 3rd Brigade 2nd Division 12th Army Corps Inscribed: Dulce et Decorum ist pro patrin man on one side A Crown for the Brave on the other side
Returned to Va 4/26/05. 19

23.   Confederate Battle Flag of Wigfall Rifles. Jeff Davis Southern Confederacy, captured by Co. F 9th Ohio Volunteers at the battle of Mill Spring, Kentucky. *Returned 3/25/05.* C *Mississippi* Ord. office. 20

24.   Confederate Flag Stars & Bars, of Flatrock Rifles, Lunenburg County, Virginia. *Returned 3/25/05.* C. Ord. Office. 21

25.   Confederate Flag, Stars & Bars. Motto: We Choose Our Own Institutions Reverse: We Collect Our Own Revenue F.R.L. 22

26.   Confederate Flag Inscribed Williamsburg and Seven Pines. This flag cannot be identified. *Supposed to have been loaned and never returned.*

27.   Confederate Battle Flag, taken in action at Willis Church Virginia, June 30th 1862 by 61st New York Volunteers Col. Frank Barlow. *Delivered to 61st N.Y. Vols. Dec. 30th 1863 By Order of the Secretary of War.*

28.   Confederate Flag, Stars & Bars, captured at Battle of Logan's Cross Roads, Kentucky, by Co. E 2nd Regiment Minnesota Volunteers. *Returned to Miss. 4/26/05.* Ord. office C. 23

29.   Confederate Flag, Stars & Bars, captured at Phillipi, Virginia, June 3rd 1861 by Lieut Wm. B. McCartney, Co. B 16th Regiment Ohio Volunteers. *Returned 3/25/05. Virginia* Ord. office. C. 24

30.   Confederate Battle Flag captured at Battle of Gettysburg, Pennsylvania, July 2nd 1863 by the 60th Regiment New York Volunteers, Green's 3rd Brigade, Geary's 2nd Division, Slocum's 12th Army Corps. *Returned to VA. 4/26/05 (See No. 22)* C. 25

31.   Confederate Battle Flag, captured from South Carolina Regiment at the Battle of Antietam, September 17th 1862 at the Stone Wall in front of the 1st Brigade, 3rd Division, 9th Army Corps, by Private Thomas Hare Co. D 89th New York Volunteers. Private Hare was afterwards killed. C. 26

32.   Confederate Battle Flag, captured at Malvern Hill, near James

River Virginia July 1st 1862, by Butterfield's Brigade, Serg't. <u>W.F. Whellock</u> 85th Pa. Volunteers, this Flag was taken from a South Carolina Regiment who piled up their dead to resist the attack of the Brigade. Ord. office C <u>27</u>

33.   <u>Confederate Battle Flag</u>, captured at the Battle of Sharpsburg, September 17th 1862 by Private <u>Isaac Thompson</u>, Co. C 20th New York State Militia. He shot the Rebel color-bearer, ran forward and brought off[sic] the colors. C. Ord. office <u>28</u>

34.   <u>Confederate Flag</u>, Stars and Bars, captured at Bristow Station Virginia October the 14th 1863, by the second Army Corps. C Ord. office <u>29</u>

35.   <u>Confederate Battle Flag</u> of the 3rd Virginia Infantry captured at Gettysburg, Pennsylvania July 2nd 1863. C <u>30</u>

36.   <u>Confederate Battle Flag</u>, of the 7th Virginia Infantry, captured by the 82nd New York Volunteers *[at Gettysburg] Returned 3/25/05* W.W. <u>31</u>

37.   <u>Confederate Battle Flag</u> of the 1st Virginia Infantry, captured by the 82nd New York Volunteers *[at Gettysburg] Returned 3/25/05* C Ord. office <u>32</u>

38.   <u>Confederate Battle Flag</u>, of 48th Georgia Infantry captured by Sergeant <u>James Wiley</u> 59th New York Volunteers. *Returned 3/25/05* C. <u>33</u>

39.   <u>Confederate Battle Flag</u>, captured by Sergeant <u>Mazzi</u> 39th New York Volunteers (Garibaldi Guards) C <u>34</u>

40.   <u>Confederate Battle Flag</u> of the 2nd Mississippi, captured by the entire Regiment of the 6th Wisconsin Volunteers, and was kept two days by Sergeant <u>Evans</u> while a prisoners in the hands of the enemy. *Medal awarded to Corporal Frank I. Waller, Co. I 6th Wis. Vol. Returned 3/25/05* W.W. Ord office <u>35</u>

41.   <u>Confederate Battle Flag</u>, of the 56th Virginia Infantry. *Returned 3/25/05* C <u>36</u>

42.   <u>Confederate Battle Flag</u> of 11th Alabama Regiment, captured at the Battle of Willis' Church, Virginia, June 30th 1862, in a charge by Colonel L.Magillon 4th Regiment Penn Reserves Corps Mead's Brigade General McCall's Division 5th Army Corps by <u>Isaac Springer</u> Co. K. of the above Regiment. Known in general orders as the Battle of New

Market Roads. *Returned 3/25/05* C *37*

43.   Confederate Battle Flag of the 1st Tennessee Regiment captured at the Battle of Gettysburg, Penn. July 3rd 1863. by the 14th Conn. Volunteers *Returned 4/26/05* C *38*

44.   Confederate Battle Flag, of the 7th North Carolina Infantry captured at the Battle of Gettysburg, Penn. July 3rd 1863 by John B. Mayberry Co. F 1st Delaware Volunteers, 2nd Brigade 3rd Division 2nd Army Corps. *Returned 3/25/05* C Ord. office *39*

45.   Confederate Battle Flag, of 38th Virginia Regiment captured at the Battle of Gettysburg Penn. July 2nd 1863 by Company G 8th Ohio Volunteers, 1st Brigade 3rd Division, 2nd Army Corps. *[Sergt Danl. Miller Co G 8th Ohio] Returned 3/25/05 40*

46.   Confederate Battle Flag, of 23rd North Carolina Regiment captured by 2nd Division 1st Army Corps at the Battle of Gettysburg Penn July 2nd 1863. *Returned 3/25/05* C *41*

47.   Confederate Battle Flag of 15th Georgia Infantry captured the Battle of Gettysburg, Penn, July 3rd 1863 by Sergeant James Thompson Company G 1st Penn. Res. Volunteers, Crawford's Division. *Returned 3/25/05* C *42*

48.   Confederate Flag, Stars and Bars, captured at the battle of Logan Field near Fishing Creek Ky. by Robert E. Bailey, Company B 10th Minn. Volunteers January 9 1862 C *43*

49.   Confederate Flag, Stars and Bars of 18th Virginia Infantry captured by 2nd Lieut. C. E. Hunt 59th New York Volunteers *Returned 3/25/05* C Ord. Office *44*

50.   Confederate Flag, Stars and Bars, captured in Zollicoffer's intrenchments, January 19 1862 by Company A 2nd Minnesota Volunteers. W.W. Ord office *45*

51.   Confederate Flag, Stars and Bars captured at the Battle of Sharpsburg September 17th 1862 by one of General Couch's command. C *46*

52.   Confederate Battle Flag, captured Bristow Station, Virginia, October 14th 1863 by the 2d Army Corps in front of the 2nd and 3rd Divisions. C *47*

53   Confederate Battle Flag, captured at Bristow Station Virginia,

Divisions. C _48_

54.   Confederate Flag, Stars and Bars C Ord. Office _49_

55.   Confederate Battle Flag, of 1861. Red and white C _50_

56.   Confederate Battle Flag, of 18th Virginia Volunteers. *Returned 3/25/05* C _51_

57.   Confederate Battle Flag, of the 16th North Carolina Infantry, captured at the Battle of Gettysburg Pa. July 3rd 1863 by the 14th Conn. Vols. *Returned 3/25/05*. F.B.L. _52_

58.   Confederate Battle Flag, of 28th Virginia Infantry. This flag cannot be identified. It is supposed to have been loaned and never returned. ~~53~~

59.   Confederate Flag, Stars and Bars. Captured at Gettysburg, Pa. July 2nd 1863. C _53_

60.   Confederate Battle Flag of the 13th Alabama Regiment, captured by Company C 1st. Delaware Volunteers. *Returned 3/25/05.* C _54_

61.   Confederate Battle Flag of the 11th Alabama Infantry, captured by the 57th New York Volunteers, Richardson's Division, Sumner's Corps. *Returned 3/25/05.* C _55_

62.   Confederate Battle Flag, captured at the Battle of Gettysburg Pen. July 2nd 1863 by the 12th New Jersey Volunteers. C _56_

63.   Confederate Battle Flag captured at the Battle of Gettysburg Penn by George H. Dore Private Co. D. 126th New York Volunteers. W.W. Ord office _57_

64.   Confederate Battle Flag of the 34th North Carolina Regiment *[captured at Gettysburg by Srgt Danl. Miller 8th Ohio] Returned 3/25/05.* C _58_

65.   Confederate Battle Flag of the 9th Virginia Infantry captured on the 3rd day of July 1863 at the Battle of Gettysburg Penn. by Private John E. Clopp Co. F, 71st Penn. Vols. *Returned 3/25/05.* C _59_

66.   Confederate Battle Flag. Captured at the battle of Gettysburg, Pennsylvania July 3rd 1863 by M. Brown Jr., Captain Co. A. 126th Regiment New York Volunteers. W.W. Ord office _60_

Regiment New York Volunteers. W.W. Ord office _60_

67.   Confederate Battle Flag of the 8th Virginia Volunteers. *Returned 3/25/05.* C _61_

68.   Confederate Battle Flag captured by the 12th Regiment New Jersey Volunteers. W.W. Ord. office _62_

69.   Confederate Battle Flag captured at the Battle of Falling Waters Va July 14th 1863. Inscribed on Flag Sharpsburg, Fredericksburg, Mechanicsville, Seven Pines, Fraziers Farm, Cedar Run, Ox Hill, Harpers Ferry, Shepardstown, Cold Harbor, Manassas, Chancellorsville. *(Identified as 47 Va) Returned 3/25/05* C _63_

70.   Confederate Battle Flag 52nd North Carolina Vols. Taken at the battle of Gettysburg Penn. July 3rd 1863 by the 14th Conn. Vols. *Returned 3/25/05,* C _64_

71.   Confederate Battle Flag. *Virginia Inf Returned 3/25/05.* _65_

72.   Confederate Battle Flag, captured at the battle of New Market Cross Roads, June 30th 1863 *[1862]* by Private Wm. Gallagher Co. F 9th Regt. Penn Reserve troops 3rd Brigade McCalls Division, from the 10th Alabama Infantry. Gallagher having killed the original bearer of the colors, took prisoner a second, who attempted to recover and raise it. Delivered to 61st N.Y.V. Dec. 30 1863 by order of the Secty of War. _66_

73.   Confederate Battle Flag of 8th Florida Regiment, captured by Sergeant Thomas Horan, 72nd N.Y. Vols. 3rd Excelsior Brigade. *Returned 3/25/05.* C _66_

74.   Confederate Battle Flag captured at the Battle of Crampton's pass, Maryland. September 14th 1862 by the 4th Regiment Vermont Volunteers. *Returned to Va., 4/26/05.* Ord. office W.W. _67_

75.   Confederate Battle Flag. W.W. Ord office _68_

76.   Confederate Battle Flag of 22nd North Carolina Infantry, captured by Private Michael McDonough 42nd New York Volunteers. Inscribed: Seven Pines, Mechanicsville, Cold Harbor, Ox Hill, Harpers Ferry, Chancellorsville, Sharpsburg, Fraziers Farm, Cedar Mountain, Manassas, Fredericksburg. *Returned 3/25/05.* _69_

77.   Confederate Battle Flag of 53rd Virginia. *Returned 3/25/05.* W.W. Ord. office. _70_

78.   Confederate Battle Flag, captured at the Battle of Gettysburg, Penn. July 3rd 1863 by corporal Navarack 39th N.Y. Volunteers. *Returned 3/25/05.* C Ord office *71*

79.   Confederate Battle Flag of the 67th *[57th]* Virginia Infantry. Captured by Private B. H. Jellison 19th Mass. Volunteers. *Returned 3/25/05.* C *72*

80.   Confederate Battle Flag of 30th Arkansas Infantry. Inscribed: Farmington, Miss. Richmond, Kentucky. Blue flag with white cross. *Returned 3/25/05.* C Ord. office *73*

81.   Confederate Battle Flag, supposed to have been captured at the Battle of Antietam September 17th 1862 by 35th Reg't. New York Vols. Colonel Lord commanding. C Ord. office *74*

82.   Confederate Battle Flag of the 53rd Virginia Infantry. June 26th 1865. loaned to Col. E. Olcott 121st N.Y. by order of the Sect'y of War.

83.   Confederate Battle Flag C *75*

84.   Virginia State Flag, captured at the Battle of Phillipi Va. June 3rd 1861. by the 14th Regiment Ohio Volunteers. Inscribed: Presented by the Ladies of Bath Va. Motto: God Protect the Right F.R.L. *76*

85.   Confederate Battle Flag, 14th Tennessee Infantry, captured at the Battle of Gettysburg Pa July 3rd 1863. by the 14th Conn. Vols. C *Returned 4/26/05. 77*

86.   Battle Flag of the 18th Alabama Regiment, captured by Lieut S. F. Josselyn, 13th Illinois Infantry. Gen'l Osterhaus' Division 15th Army Corps, at the Battle of Mission Ridge, November 25th 1863 C *Returned 3/25/05.* Ord. office *78*

87.   Confederate Battery Guidon, Blue Field, White Border, captured at the Battle of Ringold, Georgia, by Private Phillip Goettal Company B 149th N.Y. Volunteers, 3rd Brigade, 2nd Division, 12th Army Corps. C *79*

88.   Confederate Battle Flag, six pointed Stars, captured at the Battle of Missionary Ridge, November 26 1863 by the 11th Regiment Ohio Vols. Turchin's Brigade, Baird's Division, 14th Army Corps, Thomas' Department, General Grant's Army. C *80*

89.   Confederate Flag, Stars and Bars, captured at Missionary

Division 14th Army Corps November 25th 1863 C *81*

90.   Confederate Battle Flag, captured at Missionary Ridge November 26th 1863 by the 69th Ohio Volunteers, Col. M. F. Moore, Ring's Brigade, Johnson's Division. Three pieces of Ferguson's Rebel Battery were captured with it. W.W. Ord. office *82*

91.   Confederate Battle Flag, of 38th Alabama Infantry, captured at Missionary Ridge Nov. 25th 1863 by the 2nd Regt. Ohio Vols. Col A. G. McCook, Carlins Brigade, Johnson's Division, Palmer's 4th Corps, Thomas' Dept Gen'l Grant's Military Division. *Returned 3/25/05.* C.W. Ord. office *83*

92.   Confederate Flag, Stars and Bars, thirteen stars (8 pointed) three stars composing are in circle. Captured at Ringold Georgia by Private *Phillip Goettel,* Company B 149th New York Volunteers, 3rd Brigade 2nd Division 12th Army Corps November 27th 1863 C *84*

93.   Confederate Battle Flag, (Bragg's Army) captured at Lookout Mountain, November 24th 1863 by the 60th Regiment New York Volunteers, Col. Goddard, 3d Brigade, 2d Division, 12th Army Corps. C Ord. office *85*

94.   Confederate Battle Flag, (Bragg's Rebel Army) Blue ground white ball in centre captured at Lookout Mountain, Nov. 24th 1863 by Private Peter Kapperson Co. B 149th Vols 3rd Brigade 2nd Division 12th Army Corps Taken from Rebel Sergeant, who was disarmed and taken Prisoner C *86*

95.   Confederate Battle Flag, (Bragg's Rebel Army) Blue ground, white oblong centre, captured at Lookout Mountain Nov. 24th 1863. by 1st Sergt F. N. Potter Co. E 149th N.Y. Volunteers 3rd Brigade 2nd Division 12th Army Corps. This flag was captured in a hand to hand fight from a Rebel Serg't who was disarmed and taken prisoner. Serg't H[?]. F. Potter was afterwards wounded. C Ord office *87*

96.   Confederate Battle Flag, "Southern Cross" found in the intrenchments opposite Loudon Tenn by the 82nd Illinois Vols. 3d Brigade 3rd Division 11th Army Corps. The works had just been evacuated on our approach. C Ord. office *88*

97.   Confederate Flag Stars and Bars of the 26th Tennessee Volunteers, captured on prize Steamer "Cherokee" June 1863. This flag can not be identified. *Supposed to have been loaned and never returned. Query.*

98.   <u>Confederate Flag</u>, Stars & Bars   C   Ord. office *89*

99.   *Georgia*   <u>Confederate Flag</u>, Stars and Bars.   captured at Crampton's Pass, Md   Cobb's Legion, Georgia, by the 4th New Jersey Volunteers, Torbert's Brigade, Slocum's Division, Franklin's Corps. *Returned 3/25/05.* C   Ord. office *90*

100.   <u>Battle Flag</u> of the 40th Virginia Infantry, Southern Cross captured by the 1st Michigan Cavalry, at Falling Waters, Maryland July 14th 1863. *Loaned. Record obliterated in original book. Returned 3/25/05.* Ord. office

101.   <u>Confederate Flag</u>, Stars and Bars, captured at the Battle of Sharpsburg, September 17, 1862 by Private <u>Webster Carter</u>, Battery L, 1st New York Artillery. Captain Reynolds. C   Ord. office *91*

102.   *Georgia.* <u>Confederate Flag</u>, Stars and Bars (silk)(Ga. coat of Arms) *Returned 3/25/05.* S.W.   Ord. office *92*

103.   <u>Confederate Battle Flag</u>, of the Texas Brigade, captured at Sharpsburg Md September 17th 1862 by the 9th Penn Reserves. S.W. *Returned 4/26/05.* Ord. office *93*

104.   <u>Confederate Flag</u>,Stars and Bars, of the 16th Virginia Infantry, captured by the 4th Regiment New Jersey Volunteers at Crampton's Pass Md. The flag cannot be identified. *Supposed to have been loaned and never returned.*

105.   <u>Confederate Battle Flag</u>, Southern Cross. S.W.   Ord. office *94*

106.   *First Georgia Inf.* <u>Confederate Battle Flag</u>, abandoned by the enemy at the Battle of Shepardstown Bluff September 19 1862, where a portion of Griffin's Brigade, Morrell's Division, Porter's Corps(5th) forded the Potomac and carried the heights by assault. S.W. *Returned 3/31/05* Ord. office *95*

107.   <u>Confederate Battle Flag</u> of the 35th Regiment North Carolina Volunteers. *Captured by Capt. Benj. F. Youngs Co. I 1 Mich S.S. at Petersburg Va. June 17, 1864. See 51584 AGO* C   *96*

108.   <u>Confederate Flag</u>, of the 1st Georgia Regiment, Colonel Ramsey captured from General Garnets Rebel forces at the Battle of Chad River, Va. July 13 1861 by Captain <u>Blake</u> 9th Indiana Regiment Acting aid, and of the immediate party in advance of Captain Penham, of General Morris' Brigade, General McClellan's Army West Virginia S.W. *Returned*

C. MARSHALL, Major and A. D. C *3/25/05*   Ord. office *97*

109.   Confederate Flag, Stars and Bars (Silk) Marked: Independence Wilson's Invincibles W.W. Ord. office *98*

110.   Confederate Battle Flag, Hood's Texas Brigade captured by Private Samuel Johnson, 9th Penn. Reserves. C *Returned 4/26/05* Ord. office *99*

111.   Confederate Signal Flag, captured by U. S. Signal Corps, September 15th 1862. S.W. Ord. office *100*

112.   Confederate Flag, captured at Rappahannock Station, Nov. 7th 1863. The colors were stripped from the staff in order to be saved by the Color-Bearer. *Doubtless delivered the same as No. 82.*

113.   United States Flag saved from the Rebels at the surrender of Harper's Ferry, September 1862 (See no. 146 List of U.S. Flags)

114.   *Georgia.* Rebel Battle Flag captured at Knoxville Tennessee by the 9th Corps, under General Burnside form the Rebel General Longstreet's forces ata the attack on Fort Saunders. November, 1863. It was captured by Sergeant Judd company K 79th New York Volunteers. C. *Returned 4/26/05. 101*

115.   Rebel Battle Flag 16th Regt. Georgia Volunteers, captured by 9th Army Corps, under General Burnside from the Rebel General Longstreet's forces, at the attack on Fort Sanders, Tennessee, November 1863. S.W. *Returned 3/25/05. 102*

116.   Rebel Battle Flag, 16th Regt. Georgia Volunteers, captured by 9th Army Corps, under General Burnside from the Rebel General Longstreet's forces, at the attack on Fort Sanders, Knoxville, Tennessee, November 1863. C *103*

117.   Rebel Battle Flag 56th Virginia Infantry captured May 12th 1864 by Private C. W. Wilson of Co. E 4th Excelsior Regiment Birney's Division 2nd Army Corps. C *Returned 3/25/05. 104*

118.   Rebel Battle Flag *[of the 18th North Carolina]* captured by Lieut A. H. Mitchel Company A 105th Penn Volunteers, Birney's Division 2nd Army Corps, May 12th 1864. C *Returned 3/25/05 (145750 '90) 105*

119.   Rebel Battle Flag captured by Lieut. Joseph C. Paradis, Company C 5th Maine Volunteers May 10th 1864. This flag cannot be identified. Supposed to have been loaned and never returned.

120.   Rebel Battle Flag captured May 12th 1864 by Birney's Division 2nd Army Corps. *106*

121.   Rebel Battle Flag taken from the 42nd Virginia Infantry by corporal Charles L. Russell company H 73rd New York Volunteers Birney's Division, 2nd Army Corps May 12th 1864 C *Returned 3/25/ 05. 107*

122.   Rebel Battle Flag *25th Va. Vols. Returned 3/25/05* C *108*

123.   Rebel Battle Flag of 13th North Carolina Regiment captured May 6th 1864 by Sergt. S. Rough Co.. A., 14th Penn. Volunteers, Birney's Division, 2nd Army Corps. *Returned 3/25/05* C *109*

124.   Rebel Battle Flag captured by Lieut. E. Hackenberg Co. I 49th Penn Volunteers, May 13th 1864, inside the Rebel Works, after a personal struggle he succeeded in bringing the Flag off the field. C *110*

125.   Rebel Battle Flag captured at the Battle of the Wilderness, May 12th 1864 by the 1st Delaware Volunteers, Carroll's Brigade, Gibbon's Division, 2nd Army Corps. C *111*

126.   Rebel Battle Flag 30th North Carolina Infantry taken May 12th 1864 at the Battle of the Wilderness. C *Returned 3/25/05. 112*

127.   Rebel Battle Flag captured by Private M. Burke Company D 125th New York Volunteers, 3rd Brigade 1st Division 2nd Army Corps. Burke was afterwards severely wounded. C *113*

128.   Rebel Battle Flag *23rd Va. Returned 3/25/05* C *114*

129.   Rebel Battle Flag captured May 6th 1864 by 1st Sergt. J. Remp Co. H. 5th Michigan Volunteers, Birney's Division, 2nd Army Corps. *Returned 3/25/05* C *115*

130.   *55th Va.* Rebel Battle Flag captured May 6th 1864 by Sergeant W. P. Townsend Co. G 20th Ind'a Volunteers, Birney's Division 2nd Army Corps C *Returned 3/25/05. 116*

131.   *44th Va.* Rebel Battle Flag captured at the Battle of the Wilderness May 12th 1864 by Serg't Albert March Company B 64th New York Volunteers, 1st Division 2nd Army Corps C *Returned 3/25/ 05. 117*

132.   Rebel Battle Flag *118*

133.   Rebel Battle Flag, of 13th Louisiana Infantry captured May 12th 1864 by Serg't Wm. James Co. A 73rd New York Vols. and Corporal John L. Reynolds Co. F 4th Excelsior Regiment, Birney's Division, 2nd Army Corps. Serg't James was afterwards killed. C *Returned 3/25/05.* *119*

134.   Rebel Battle Flag 28th North Carolina Regiment captured May 12th 1864 by Corpl. J. M. Kindig company H 63rd Penn. Vols. Birney's Division, 2nd Army Corps. C *Returned 3/25/05.* *120*

135.   Rebel Battle Flag of 1st North Carolina Regiment captured by Private George W. Harris Co. B 148th Penn. Vols. 4th Brigade 1st Division 2nd Army Corps in the charge made by the 2nd Corps on the morning of May 12th 1864. C *Returned 3/25/05.* *121*

136.   Rebel Battle Flag captured May 12th 1864 at the Battle of the Wilderness by 1st Lieut. Charles McInaly 69th Regiment Penn. Vet. Volunteers. C   *122*

137.   Rebel Battle Flag of 4th Virginia Infantry taken May 12th 1864 in the Battle of the Wilderness. C *123 Returned 3/25/05*

138.   Rebel Battle Flag taken by 152nd New York Volunteers. C *124*

139.   Rebel Battle Flag of 48th Miss. Infty captured at the Battle of the Wilderness May 12th 1864 by the 12th N.J. Vols., Carroll's Brigade. C *Returned 3/25/05*   *125*

140.   Rebel Battle Flag 44th Georgia Regiment, captured May 10th 1864 by the 43rd New York Volunteers, 3rd Brigade, 2nd Div. 1st Army Corps C *Returned 3/25/05   126*

141.   Rebel Battle Flag captured by Captain J.C. Briscau A.D.C. to Major General D. B. Birney 3rd Division 2nd Army Corps C   *127*

142.   Virginia State Flag captured June 3rd 1864 by corporal Francis Bigley company D 7th New York Artillery, 4th Brigade 1st Division 2nd Army Corps at the Battle of the Wilderness C *128*

143.   Rebel Flag Blue ground with red cross stripes captured at the Battle of the Wilderness June 6th 1864 by Birney's Division 2nd Army Corps This flag resembles the British Union Jack. C *129*

144.   Rebel Flag Blue with white border and white Ball in the centre

taken from the Rebels before Petersburg VA. June 1864 by the 9th Army Corps. C *130*

145.   Rebel Flag of 44th Tennessee Infantry, white border and white ball in centre, captured June 1864 by the 48th Penn. Volunteers 9th Army Corps from the Rebels before Petersburg, Va. *Robert A. Reid Co. G. 48th Pa. Vols.* C *Returned 4/26/06 131*

146.   Rebel Battle Flag, Southern Cross, captured June 1864 from the Rebels before Petersburg Va. by the 9th Army Corps. C *132*

147.   Rebel Battle Flag, Southern Cross, captured June 1864 from the Rebels before Petersburg Va. by the 9th Army Corps. C *133* Ord. office

148.   One Half Confederate Battle Flag captured from Rebel Infantry in an engagement near Malvern Hill July 28th 1864 by Private George Funk Company K 6th New York Cavalry 2nd Brig. 1st Div. Army of the Potomac June 26th 1865. Loaned to W.H. Ryder by Order of the Sect'y of War (s)

149.   Confederate Battle Flag of the 28th North Carolina Regiment captured in an engagement near Malvern Hill, July 28th 1864 by Private Samuel L. Mallick Company I 9th New York Cavalry 2nd Brigade 1st Cavalry Division Army of the Potomac. *Returned 3/25/05 134* Ord. office

150.   Confederate Battle Flag 18th North Carolina Regiment captured in an engagement near Malvern Hill, Va. July 28th 1864 by Private Timothy Connors Co. C 1st U.S. Cavalry, Reserve Brigade, 1st Cav. Division, Army of the Potomac. Presented by General Torbert. *Returned 3/25/05 135* C

151.   Confederate Battle Flag captured at Petersburg Va. July 30th 1864 by the 14th New York Heavy Artillery 9th Army Corps C *136*

152.   Confederate Battle Flag captured by Capt. Wright 43rd U.S. Colored Troops at the battle of Petersburg Va. July 30th 1864 Ferrero's Division 9th Army Corps C *137*

153.   Confederate Battle Flag captured by 50th Penn. Vet. Volunteers 2nd Brigade, 3rd Division, 9th Army Corps C *Returned 3/25/05 47th Va. Vols 138*

154.   Confederate Battle Flag C *139*

155.   Confederate Battle Flag. C *140*

156.   Confederate Battle Flag. C *141*

157.   Confederate Battle Flag, captured by the 56th Penn. Vet. Vols. Col Hoffman 2nd Brigade 4th Division 5th Army Corps August 19th 1864 at the battle of Globe Tavern, near Weldon R.R. Virginia C *55th North Carolina. Returned 3/25/05. 142*

158.   Remnants of the Battle Flag of the 16th Mississippi Captured by Captain Horace Ellis Co. A 7th Wisconsin Volunteers, General Bragg's Brigade, Cutler's Division, 5th Army Corps. C *Returned 3/25/05 143*

159.   Confederate Battle Flag, of the 27th S.C. Regiment, captured by Private F. C. Anderson Co. A. 18th Mass. Battalion. S.W. Ord. office. *Returned 4/26/05 144*

160.   Confederate Battle Flag, (silk) 24th N.C. Volunteers, captured August 21st 1864 by Private J.D. Read 11th Penn. Vet. Volunteers. S.W. Ord. office *Returned 3/25/05 145*

161.   Confederate Battle Flag, (silk) captured by Serg't David H. Schofield 5th New York Cavalry, October 19th 1864. S.W. *Returned 4/26/05. 146*

162.   Confederate Battle Flag, captured by Serg't W. A. Haugh Co. E. 8th Indiana 4th Brigade 2nd Division 19th Army Corps. S.W. Ord. office *147*

163.   Colors of the 12th North Carolina Inft'y captured by Serg't. E.D. Woodbury Co. E. 1st Vermont Cavalry. C *Returned 3/25/05 148*

164.   Confederate Battle Flag, captured by Corporal David P. Reigler Co. F 87th Penn. Volunteers 1st Brig. 3rd Div 6th A.C. Oct. 19th 1864 C Ord. office *149*

165.   Confederate Battle Flag, captured from the enemy at Fisher's Hill Va. Sept. 22nd 1864 by Private George G. Moore Co. D. 11th West Va. Vols. 1st Division of the Army of West Virginia. S.W. *150*

166.   Confederate Battle Flag, captured by Private Richard Taylor Co. E. 18th Indiana October 19th 1864 from a wounded rebel. C *151*

167.   Confederate Battle Flag, captured by the 14th Penn. Cavalry October 26th 1864 in Luray Valley. S.W. Ord. office *Returned to VA.,*

4/26/05 152

168.   Confederate Colors, captured by James M. Compston Co. D 71st Ohio Regiment, 2nd Brigade 2nd Division, Army of West Virginia. This flag cannot be identified. Supposed to have been loaned, and never returned.

169.   Confederate Battle Flag, captured by Captain Edwards, 1st Veteran Cav. October 19th 1864. S.W. Ord. office *153*

170.   Confederate Battle Flag, captured by Private Phillip B. Daybutt, Co.A 2nd Mass. Cavalry, Luray, Virginia. September 24th 1864. S.W. Ord. office *[6th Va. Cav.] Returned 3/25/05. 154*

171.   Confederate Battle Flag, of the 32nd Batt. Va. Cavalry. Captured by Private Edward Handford Co. H. 2nd U.S. Cavalry near Woodstock Va. October 9th 1864. S.W. Ord. office *Returned 3/25/05. 155*

172.   Confederate Battle Flag, captured by General Sheridan's forces October 19th 1864 *Sept. 13/64 from 8 S.C. Infty.* S.W. Ord. office *Returned 3/25/05. 156*

173.   Confederate Battle Flag, of the 18th Georgia Infantry, captured by Private Hedrick Crocker Co. M. 6th Michigan Cavalry 1st Brigade, 1st Division, Cavalry Corps. S.W. Ord. office *Returned 3/25/05. 157*

174.   Confederate Battle Flag. *No History* S.W. Ord office

175.   Confederate Battle Flag, captured August 16th 1864 near Front Royal, Virginia, by Sergeant H. J. Murray, Co. B 4th New York Cav. and Private Frank Leslie Co. B same regiment from the 3rd Virginia Cavalry. S.W. Ord. office *Returned 3/25/05 159*

176.   Virginia State Flag captured September 19th 1864 near Winchester Va. by Private George Reynolds C. M 9th New York Cavalry 2nd Brigade, 1st Cavalry Division. S.W. Ord. office *Returned 3/25/05. 160*

177.   Confederate Battle Flag, captured at Fisher's Hill, Virginia September 22nd 1864, by Private John Creed Co. D. 23rd Illinois Veteran Volunteers, 1st Division, Army of West Virginia. S.W. Ord. office *161*

178.   Confederate Battle Flag, S.W. Ord. office *162*

179.   Confederate Battle Flag, S.W. Ord. office *No History 163*

180.   Confederate Battle Flag, captured by Private James Conner, Col. E 43rd N.Y. Volunteers September 22nd 1864 at Fisher's Hill Va. S.W. Ord. office *Supposed to belong to 2nd La. Inf.* 164

181.   Confederate Battle Flag, captured September 19th 1864 near Winchester Va. by Corporal Chester B. Bonon Co. I 1st N.Y. Dragoons, 2nd Brigade, 1st Cavalry Division. S.W. Ord. office *165*

182.   A part of a Confederate Flag, captured during the charge of Hancock's Corps, near Spottsylvania Va. May 12th 1864 by Lieut. Franenburgh commanding Co B 20th Indiana Vet. Volunteers. C *166*

183.   Confederate Battle Flag, of the 6th Virginia Infantry, captured July 30th 1864 by Cpl. Franklin Hogan Co. A. 45th Penn. Volunteers. C *167*

184.   Confederate Battle Flag, captured by Private J. Parks Co. A 9th New York Cavalry, Devin's Brigade 1st Cav. Division. C. *168*

185.   Confederate Battle Flag, captured by Col. George M. Lane 116th N.Y. Vols. October 19th 1864 at Cedar Creek Va. This flag cannot be identified. Supposed to have been loaned and never returned

186.   Confederate Battle Flag, of a *(the 50th)* Va. Regiment, captured in the Wilderness by Private John H. Opel, Co. G 7th Indiana Volunteers 1st Brigade 4th Division 5th Army Corps. C *Returned 3/25/05.* 169

187.   Colors of the 44th Georgia Infantry, captured in the Battle of Cedar Creek October 19th 1864 by chief Bugler, S.M. Wills 6th N.Y. Cavalry, 2nd Brigade, 1st Division. S.W. Ord. office. *Returned 3/25/ 05.* 170

188.   *North Carolina.* State Colors captured by Private James Sweeney Co. A 1st Veteran Cavalry, October 19th 1864. S.W. Ord. office *171*

189.   Confederate Battle Flag, of the 47th North Carolina Regiment captured at the battle of Hatcher's Run, Oct. 27th 1864 by Serg't David Murphy 19th Mass. Vols. 1st Brigade, 2nd Division 2nd Army Corps, commanded by Brig.Gen'l, Eagan. C. *Returned 3/25/05.* 172

190.   Flag of the 46th Virginia Regiment, recently commanded by Governor Wm. Smith, taken April 6th 1862 at Warrenton Va. C *Returned 3/25/05.* 173

191.   Confederate Battle Flag, of the 26th North Carolina Regiment captured at the Battle of Hatcher's Run, October 27th 1864 by Serg't Alonzo Smith 7th Michigan Vols. 1st Brigade 2nd Division 2nd Army Corps, commanded by Brig General Egan. C *Returned 3/25/05. 174*

192.   Confederate Battle Flag, *[2nd La.] captured May 12th 1864 near Spottsylvania Virginia by Serg't C. H. Fusnacht, Co. A 99th Penn. Vols.* C Returned 3/25/05. *175*

193.   Remnant of a Confederate Battle Flag, captured May 12th 1864 near Spottsylvania, Virginia. C *176*

194.   Battle Flag of the 6th Alabama Regiment captured by B. F. Davis 22nd Mass. Volunteers 2nd Brigade 1st Div. 5th Army Corps. S.W. Ord. office *Returned 3/25/05. 177.*

195.   Confederate Battle Flag, captured by Sergeant Henry M. Fose[?] Co. M. 5th Michigan Cavalry 1st Brigade 1st Division at Winchester Va. September 19th 1864. S.W. Ord. office *178*

196.   Confederate Colors Stars and Bars, captured by Private Gabriel Cole Company I 5th Michigan Cavalry, 1st Brigade, 1st Division, Winchester, September 19th 1864. S.W. Ord. office *46th Va. See 522902 AGO 179*

197.   Confederate Battle Flag, of the 2nd Virginia Infantry, Stonewall's old Brigade, Early's Corps, Thirteen battles inscribed upon it. Captured by the 34th Wisc. Volunteers 3rd Brigade 1st Division 6th Army Corps at the Battle of Winchester September 19th 1864. C *Returned 3/25/ 05. 180*

198.   Colors of the 36th Virginia Volunteers, captured September 19th 1864 near Winchester Va. by Patrick McEnroe, Private company D. 6th New York Cavalry, 2nd Brigade 1st Cavalry Division. S.W. Ord. office *Returned 3/25/05. 181*

199.   Confederate Battle Flag, captured by Private O. S. Muldurn, Co. I William Smith Co. D and Kelly Co. H 6th New York Cavalry, near Front Royal, Virginia, August 16th 1864. S.W. Ord. office *182*

200.   Confederate Battle Flag, captured September 19th 1864, near Winchester, Virginia, by George E. Mach, Farrier, Co. I 6th N.Y. Cavalry, 2nd Brigade, 1st Cavalry Division. S.W. Ord. office *183*

201.   Confederate Battle Flag, C. *184*

202.   Flag. Supposed to be a Rebel signal flag, captured in the Shenandoah Valley, by a portion of General Sheridan's army, September 1864. C. Ord. office *185*

203.   Confederate Battle Flag, captured near Winchester Va. by Commissary Sergeant Andrew J. Lorish 1st New York Dragoons Sept. 19th 1864 S.W. *Virginia Regt Returned 3/25/05. 186*

204.   Confederate National Flag, found in the knapsack of a dead Rebel in the Wilderness, May 6th 1864. F.R. *187*

205.   Black Flag, captured within the Rebel Lines, near North Mountain, Md., August 1st 1864 by Detective C.H. March of the Middle Department. C *188*

206.   Colors of the 8th and 19th Alabama Regiments. C. *Returned 3/25/05. 189*

207.   Battle Flag of the 48th Virginia Infantry, captured at the battle of the Wilderness, May 5th 1864 by Lieut. Col. Albert M. Edwards, 24th Michigan Volunteers. C *Returned 3/25/05. 190*

208.   Flag of the 19th Georgia Regiment captured December 13th 1862 by Private Jacob Cart, Co. A 7th Penn Reserves Corps. C Ord. office *Returned 3/25/05. 191*

209.   Battle Flag of the 44th Mississippi, captured by Corporal Luther B. Kaltenback, Co. F 12th Iowa Infantry, at the Battle of Brentwood Hills, near Nashville, Tennessee, Dec. 16th 1864. C *Returned 3/25/05. 192*

210.   Rebel Flag of Chalmer's Division. captured December 24th 1864 near Richland Creek Tennessee, by Corp. Harrison Collins Co. A. 1st Ten. Cavalry. The Corporal determined to have the Flag, led a charge, Killed a Major, routed his men and secured the Flag. C. *193*

211.   Battle Flag of the 24th La. Infantry, captured by 1st Lieut. Wm. S. Simmons Co. C 11th Mo.Vols. at the Battle of Brentwood Hills, near Nashville Tennessee December 16th 1864. C. *Returned 3/25/05. 194*

212.   Rebel Battle Flag, captured by 1st Lieut. Charles H. McClary Co. C 72nd Ohio Volunteers, at the Battle of Brentwood Hills, near Nashville, Tennessee, December 16th 1864. C. *Florida —Returned 4/26/05. 195*

213.   Rebel Battle Flag, captured by 1st Lieut. and Adjutant, Thomas

P. Gere, 5th Minn. Volunteers, at the Battle of Brentwood Hills, near Nashville, Tenn. December 13th 1864. C *[4th Miss] Returned 3/25/ 05. 196*

214.   Rebel Battle Flag, captured by Serg't Wm. Garrett Co. C. 41st Ohio Vl. Infantry at the battle of Brentwood Hills, December 16th 1864. C *197*

215.   Rebel Battle Flag, captured by Private W.F. Moore Co. C 117th Ill. Infantry at the Battle of Nashville, Tenn. Dec. 16th 1864. C. *198*

216.   Rebel Battle Flag, captured by Private G. W. Welch, Co. A 11th Mo. Vet. Vols Inf'ty at the Battle of Brentwood Hills, Tenn. Dec. 16th 1864. C *199*

217.   *Missouri Inf.* Rebel Battle Flag, captured by Sergeant Alfred Ransbottom Co. K. 97th O.V.I. at the Battle of Brentwood Station near Nashville Tenn. November 30th 1864. C. *Returned 3/25/05 200*

218.   Remnant of a Confederate Battle Flag, captured by 1st Lieut. Oliver Colwell Co. A. 95th O.V.I. at the Battle of Brentwood Hills, near Nashville Tenn. December 16th 1864. C *201*

219.   Rebel Battle Flag, captured by George Stokes, Private Co. D. 122nd Ill. Vols. at the Battle of Richland Creek, near Nashville Tennessee Dec 15th 1864. C. *202*

220.   Flag of Branchard's Battery, captured by Private Wm. May, Co. H 32nd Iowa Infantry, 2nd Brigade 2nd Division, Detachment of the Army of Tennessee, at the Battle of Brentwood Hills near Nashville, Tennessee, December 16th 1864. C. *[Louisiana] Returned 3/25/05. 203*

221.   Battle Flag of the 6th Florida, captured by Private Otis Smith Co. G. 96th O.V.I. at the Battle of Brentwood Hills near Nashville Tennessee, December 16th 1864. C *Returned 3/25/05. 204*

222.   Battle Flag of the 5th Alabama Regiment, captured by the 111th Penn. Vols. 2nd Brigade, 2nd Division, 12th A.C. at Chancellorsville, VA. May 3rd 1863. Ord. office *See No. 2 Returned 3/ 25/05.*

223.   Battle Flag of the 3rd Texas Cavalry, capture by the 3rd Cavalry Division and 1st and 2nd Brigade of the 2nd Cav. Division under command of Brig. Gen. Kilpatrick on raid on Macon Railroad August 20th 1864. C *205*

224.   Battle Flag of 12th Louisiana Infantry, captured July 20th 1864 at the Battle of Peachtree Creek, Ga. by the 105th Regt. Ill Vols. 20th A.C. Army of the Cumberland. C *Returned 3/25/05.* *206*

225.   Battle Flag of the 6th Regiment Ky. Vols. captured by Co. G 10th Regt. Michigan Vet. Vols. 1st Brigade 2nd Division 14th A.C. at the Battle of Jonesboro September 1st 1864 with the Regimental Colonel Lee. S.W. Ord. office *207*

226.   Confederate Battle Flag captured by the Cavalry Corps, Military Div. of the Mississippi at the Battle of Richland Creek Dec. 16th 1864. F.R. *208*

227.   *Ala.* Flag of the 3rd Confederate Regiment, captured September 1st 1864 by the 2nd Brigade, 2nd Division 14th Army Corps. C *Returned 4/26/05.* *209*

229.   Battle Flag 1st Miss. Regt. captured at Peachtree Creek, July 20th 1864, by Private Dennis Buckley Co. G 136th New York Volunteers 20th Army Corps, Army of the Cumberland. C *Returned 3/25/05.* *210*

228.   Flag of Swetts Battery, captured at Jonesboro September 1st 1864 by the 16th Regiment Illinois Vet. Vols. 3rd Division 14th A.C., Army of the Cumberland. C *211*

230.   Confederate Battle Flag, captured by the Cavalry command, Military Division of the Mississippi. C Ord. office *212*

231.   Flag of Key's Battery, captured by Gilbert S. Fleming Co. B 52nd Regt. Ohio Vols. Jonesboro September 1st 1864. C *Returned 3/25/05.* *213*

232.   Battle Flag of the 38th Regiment Alabama Volunteers, captured at the Battle of Resaca, May 15th 1864 by Captain Box Co. D. 27th Indiana Vols. 2nd Brigade, 1st Division 20th Army Corps, Army of the Cumberland Major General Thomas Commanding. C Ord. office *Returned 3/25/05.* *214*

233.   Rebel Battle Flag captured at the Battle of Resaca, Georgia, May 15th 1864 by Corpl. H. Syrell Co. H 5th Ohio Vet. Vols. at the "Sunken" Battery in front of the 1st Brigade 2nd Division, 20th A.C. Forwarded by Brig. Gen. John W. Geary Comdg. 2nd Division, 20th A.C. C *Returned 4/26/05.* *215*

234.   General Early's Headquarters Flag, Confederate National

Standard captured in Battle at Waynesboro Va. March 2nd 1865 by Captain <u>Christopher C. Bruton</u> Co. C. 22nd New York Cavalry, 2nd Brigade, 3rd Cavalry Division Bt. Maj. Gen. George A. Custar Commdg. S.W. *Returned to VA., 4/26/05.* <u>*216*</u>

235.   <u>Battle Flag</u> 33rd Miss. Regt. captured by the 26th Regiment Wisconsin Volunteers, at Peachtree Creek Ga. July 20th 1864. 20th Corps Army of the Cumberland. S.W. Ord. office *Returned 3/25/05.* <u>*217*</u>

236.   <u>Confederate National Standard</u>, captured at the Battle of Resaca May 15th 1864 by the Army of the Cumberland, Major General Thomas Commanding. C Ord. office <u>*218*</u>

237.   <u>Colors of the Benjamin Infantry</u>, organized April 24th 1861, Clayton Co. Georgia. "Strike for your Alters and your Firesides." Captured by 3rd Cavalry Division and 1st and 2nd Brigades 2nd Cavalry Division Department of the Cumberland under command of Brig. Gen. Kilpatrick on Raid on Macon Railroad August 20th 1864. C *Returned 3/25/05. Georgia* <u>*219*</u>

238.   <u>Rebel Battle Flag</u>, captured by Sergeant <u>Levi Schoemaker</u> Co. A. 1st Va. Cavalry on the 12th of November 1864 in an engagement near Ninnevah Va. Brig. Gen. W. H. Powell commanding 2nd Division S.W. Ord. office *Returned to VA., 4/26/05.* <u>*220*</u>

239.   Rebel Battle Flag, taken (near Willis') in action June 30th 1862 by the 61st New York Volunteers, <u>Col. Frank Barlow</u>. C <u>*221*</u>

240.   <u>Confederate Colors</u> captured by <u>Corporal Newton H. Hall</u> Co. I 104th O.V.I. 1st Brigade 3rd Division 23rd Army Corps. S.W. <u>*222*</u>

241.   <u>Confederate Colors</u> captured by <u>Corporal Nemton H. Hall</u> Co. I 104th O.V.I. 1st Brigade 3rd Division 23rd Army Corps. S.W. Ord. office *[Nov. 30/64]* <u>*223*</u>

242.   <u>Flag of the 16th Alabama Regiment</u>, captured by <u>A. Greenawalt</u> Co. G 104th O.V.I. 1st Brigade, 3rd Division 23rd A.C. S.W. Ord. office *[Nov.30/64] Returned 3/25/05.* <u>*224*</u>

243.   <u>Captured by Major Edward Mutterine</u>, commanding 175th Ohio Vol. Infantry S.W. Ord. office <u>*225*</u>

244.   *Confed. Sig. Flag.* <u>Captured by Private S. H. Ricksecer</u> Co. D. 104th Ohio Volunteer Infantry 1st Brig. 3rd Division 23rd A.C. S.W. Ord. office *[Nov. 30/64]* <u>*226*</u>

245.   Rebel Battle Flag captured by John H. Brown, Co. D. 12th Ky Infantry. S.W. Ord. office. *227*

246.   Rebel Colors captured by Captain G. V. Kelly 104th O.V.I. 1st Brig. 3rd Division 23rd A.C. at the Battle of Franklin November 30th 1864. S.W. Ord. office S.W. *228*

247.   Flag of the 81st Pa. Vols. Returned to Major Ja. H. Mitchel 81st Pa. Vols.

248.   Remains of the Colors belonging to the 1st U.S. Sharpshooters. Turned over to the War Department by the desire of the Regiment. W.W. *Should be with U.S. flags*

249.   Rebel Battle Flag captured in Battle at Wainsboro Va. March 2nd 1865 by Private M. Crowley Co. A. 22nd New York Cavalry, 2nd Brigade, 3rd Cavalry Division Bvt. Maj. Genl. Geo. A. Custar commanding S/W/ *229*

250.   Battle Flag, captured in Battle at Wainsboro, Va. by Private John Miller Co. A. 8th New York Cavalry 2nd Brigade 3rd Cavalry Division. Bvt. major General Geo. A. Custar commdg. S.W. Ord. office *230*

251.   This Flag was captured in Battle at Wainsboro, Virginia, March 2nd 1865 by Corporal Harry Harvey, Co. A. 22nd New York Cavalry, 2nd Brigade 3rd Cav. Division. Bvt. Maj. Gen'l Geo. A. Custar Commdg. S.W. Ord. office *231*

252.   Battle Flag captured in Battle at Wainsboro Va. March 2nd 1865 by Private W. Carman Co. H. 1st New York Cav 3rd Brigade 3rd Division Bvt. Maj. General Geo. A. Custar Commdg. S.W. *232*

253.   Battle Flag, captured in Battle at Wainsboro Virginia March 2nd 1865 by Private G. Ladd Co. A. 22nd New York Cav. 2nd Brigade 3rd Cavalry Division Bvt. Maj. Gen. Geo. A. Custar commdg. S.W. *Peter Owen, Co. A. 1 N.Y. Cav. 233*

254.   Battle Flag, captured in Battle at Wainsboro Virginia March 2nd 1865 by Private G. Ladd Co. A. 22nd New York Cav. 2nd Brigade 3rd Cavalry Division Bvt. Maj. Gen. Geo. A. Custar commdg. S.W. *No state. Returned 3/25/05 234*

255.   Battle Flag, captured at Charlottesville, Virginia, March 5th 1865 by Sergt. Richard Boury Co. C. 1st.Va. Cav. 2nd and 3rd Division.

Bvt. Major General Geo. A. Custar Commdg. S.W. *Returned 3/25/05.*
<u>235</u>

256.   This Flag, captured in Battle at Wainsboro Va. March 2nd 1865
by <u>Sergeant C. W. Galsun,</u> Co. G. 8th New York Cavalry 2nd Brigade 3rd
Cavalry Division Bvt. Maj. Genl. Geo. A. Custar commdg. S.W. <u>236</u>

257.   Battle Flag, captured at Wainsboro Va. March 2nd 1865 by
<u>Lieut. A. Kuder,</u> Co. G. 8th New York Cavalry 2nd Brigade 3rd Cavalry
Division Bvt. Maj. Genl. Geo. A. Custar commdg. S.W. <u>237</u>

258.   Battle Flag, captured at Wainsboro Va. March 2nd 1865 by
<u>Major Hartwell Campson,</u> 8th New York Cavalry 2nd Brigade 3rd
Cavalry Division Bvt. Maj. Genl. Geo. A. Custar commdg. S.W. <u>238</u>

259.   Battle Flag of the 41st Alabama Volunteers, captured by Corp.
F. W. Lutes, Company C. 111th New York Volunteers in the charge of
the enemy upon our line before Petersburg March 31st 1865. S.W.
Returned March 25, 1905. <u>239</u>

260.   Flag captured in the Battle at Wainsboro Virginia March 2nd
1865 by Lieut. <u>Robert Niven</u> 8th New York Cavalry 2nd Brigade, 3rd
Cav. Division Bvt. Major General Custar Commanding. S.W. <u>240</u>

261.   Flag captured in the Battle at Wainsboro Virginia March 2nd
1865 by Lieut. <u>Robert Niven</u> 8th New York Cavalry 2nd Brigade, 3rd
Cav. Division Bvt. Major General Custar Commanding. S.W. <u>241</u>

262.   Flag captured in the Battle at Wainsboro Virginia March 2nd
1865 by Sergeant <u>Daniel Kelly</u> Co., G. 8th New York Cavalry 2nd
Brigade, 3rd Cav. Division Bvt. Major General Custar Commanding.
S.W. <u>242</u>

263.   Flag of the 2nd Georgia Battery, captured by <u>Patrick McCran,</u>
Co. C. 3rd Md. This flag has 28 bullet holes in it and 3 through the staff.
C *Returned 3/25/05.* <u>243</u>

264.   Staff and Remnant of Flag. S.W. <u>244</u>

265.   Staff and Remnant of Flag S.W. *No staff found* <u>245</u>

266.   Virginia State Colors *No history* <u>246</u>

267.   Confederate Battle Flag. S.W. <u>247</u>

268.   Confederate Battle Flag, captured by Private <u>McDonald</u> Co. L

1st Connecticut Artillery, near Fort Stedman, March 25th 1865. S.W. *Georgia. Returned 4/26/05. 248*

269.   Remnant of Battle Flag. S.W. *249*

270.   Remnant of Battle Flag. S.W. *250*

271.   Battle Flag of the 26th S.C. Volunteers, "Secessionville" June 16th 1862. *April 26th 1865 Loaned to W. H. Ryden. By order of General Nichols.*

272.   *Ala.* Rebel Battle Flag, captured on the left of the Watkins House March 25th 1865 by Private George W. Tompkins Co. F 124th New York Volunteers, 1st Brigade, 3rd Division, 2nd Army Corps.   C *Returned 4/26/05. 251*

273.   Rebel Battle Flag, captured April 1st 1865, by Sergeant Robert F. Shipley Co. K 140th New York Volunteers. C *(9 Virginia) Returned 3/25/05. 252*

274.   Flag of the 14th Va. Regiment, captured by Sergeant H. A. Delavie Co. I 11th Penn. Volunteers 2nd Brigade 3rd Division 5th Army Corps, at the Battle of Five Forks, Va. April 1st 1865. C *Returned 3/25/05. 253*

275.   Rebel Battle Flag, captured April 1st 1865 by Private David Edwards Co. K 146th New York Volunteers. C *(24th North Carolina) 254*

276.   Colors of the 30th Virginia, captured by Private George Shapp Co. E 191st Penn. Vols. who being on the skirmish line, and seeing the enemy rallying a line of Battle on the Colors, sprang forward along with a dismounted Cavalryman and demanded a surrender. A Rebel Officer called to his men to shoot the two Yankees, whereupon the Cavalryman was shot dead.

Private Shapp shot the Rebel Officer and seized the Colors, for the bearer, at the instant the Skirmish line of the 3rd Brigade 2nd Division 5th Army Corps charged on the line of Battle, fled. C *Returned 3/25/05. 255*

277.   Flag of the 16th South Carolina Volunteers, was captured by Capt. J. W. Scott Co. D. 157th Penn. Vols. It was taken from the hands of the Color bearer on the line during the engagement of April 1st 1865 at Five Forks, Va. C *Returned 3/25/05. 256*

278.   Rebel Battle Flag, captured April 1st 1865 by 1st Sergeant

Thomas J. Murphy, Co. G. 146th New York Volunteers. C *257*

279.   Rebel Battle Flag, captured April 1st 1865 by Corporal August Rauss*[?]* Co. H 15th New York Heavy Artillery. C *258*

280.   Remnant of Rebel Flag, captured by Private L. F. Brest Co. D 57th Penn. Vols. at Sailor's Creek April 6th 1865. C *259*

281.   Rebel Battle Flag, captured by A. E. Fernald, 20th Maine Vols. 3rd Brig. 1st Division 5th Army Corps at the Battle of Five Forks, April 1st 1865. S.W. *Returned to Va., 4/26/05. 260*

282.   Rebel Flag, captured by Private Alderbert Everson Co. G. 1st. Md. Vet. Vols. 2nd Brigade 2nd Division 5th A.C. April 1st 1865. S.W. *261*

283.   Rebel Battle Flag, captured April 1st 1865 at the Battle of Five Forks Va. by Private C. Gardiner, Co. E 32nd Mass. Vols. 1st Batt. S.S. 3rd Brigade 1st Division 5th A.C. April 1st 1865. C Ord. office *262*

284.   Rebel Flag, captured by Private Joseph Stenard Co. G 1st Md.. Vet. Vols. 2nd Brigade 2nd Division 5th A.C. April 1st 1865. C *263*

285.   Rebel Flag, captured by J. W. Johnson Co. B 12th Reg't West Va. Infantry April 2nd 1865 at Hatcher's Run Va. C Ord. office *264*

286.   Rebel Flag, captured by Gordon's Corps. C *265*

287.   Rebel Flag, captured by 1st Lieut. Jacob Kough Co. G 7th Md. Vols. 2nd Brigade 2nd Division 5th A.C. at the Battle of Five Forks April 1st 1865. C *266*

288.   Rebel Flag, of the 35th Georgia Reg't Heth's Division Longstreet's Corps. C *Returned 3/25/05. 267*

289.   *8th Mississippi* Rebel Flag, captured by Private Richard Mangrum 148th New York Vols. from the 8th Miss. Reg't. on the 2nd April 1865 at the time of the advance of the skirmish line of the 4th Brigade 1st Division 21st A.C. on the Enemy's Works, about 300 prisoners and five guns with caissons etc. complete were captured at the same time. C *Returned 3/25/05. 268*

290.   Rebel Flag, captured by the skirmish line of the 1st Brigade 1st Division 24th A.C. April 7th 1865 during the engagement with the rear Guard of Gen'l Lee's Army of Northern Virginia, at Rush River, near Farmville, Va. C *269*

291.   *42nd Mississippi* Rebel Flag, captured by C. A. Reeder Co. G 12th Regiment West Va Inft'y April 2nd 1865 at Hatcher's Run Va. S.W. *(42 Miss) Returned 3/25/05.* 270

292.   Hospital Flag captured by Lewis Cook Co. A 1st New Jersey Cav. Residence Clinton Co. N.Y. S.W. 271

293.   Rebel Battle Flag, captured in Battle at Farms Cross Roads April 5th 1865 by Serg't James P. Landis, Chief Bugler 1st Pa Cavalry, 1st Brigade 2nd Cav. Division Bvt. Maj. Genl. Davis commdg. *Loaned to Bvt. Maj. Gen'l Davis May 23 ( ) By order of Gen. Nichols*

294. *26 GA* Rebel Flag, of the 76th Georgia Regiment captured in Battle at Sailor's Creek April 6th 1865. by Corporal Emisire Shahan Co. A. 1st Va. Vet. Vols. Cavalry 3rd Brigade 3rd Cav. Division Bvt. Maj. General Geo. A. Custar Commdg. E.W. *Returned 3/25/05* 272

295.   Rebel Flag, captured by Lieut Randolph Biddell Co. I 61st New York Volunteers April 6th 1865. E.W. 273

296.   Battle Flag of the 27th Virginia Infty. captured in Battle at Sailor's Creek April 6th 1865 by Private W. F. Holmes Co. A 3rd Inda. Vol. Cavalry. Escort Co. Hd Qrs. 3rd Cav. Division Bvt. Maj. General George A. Custar Commdg. E.W. *Returned 3/25/05.* 274

297.   Rebel Flag, captured by Private George Floyd Co. A. 122nd Ohio Vols. at the Battle of Petersburg Va. April 2nd 1865. E.W. 275

298.   Confederate Standard, captured by Corporal A.F. Harpies Co. H 17th Maine Vols. April 6th 1865 at Sailor's Creek. E.W. 276

299.   Rebel Battle Flag, captured in Battle at Sailor's Creek, April 6th 1865 by Private Wm. Sheppard Co. A 3rd Indiana Cavalry. Escort to Hd Qrs 3rd Cav. Division, Bvt. Maj. Gen'l Geo. A. Custar Commdg. E.W. 277

300.   Rebel Flag, of General Kershaw's Hd Qrs captured in Battle at Sailor's Creek April 6th 1865 by Corp'l Smith Larimore Co. G. 2nd Ohio Vet. Vol. Cav. 1st Brigade 3rd Cav. Division Bvt. Maj. Gen'l Geo. A. Custar Commdg. E.W. 278

301.   Rebel Battle Flag, of the 38th Va. Infantry, captured in Battle of Sailors Creek April 6th 1865 by Corp'l John B. Hughey Co. L 2nd Ohio Vet. Vols. 1st Brigade 3rd Cav. Division General Custar Commdg. E.W. *Returned 3/25/05.* 279

302.   Battle Flag of the 9th Virginia Infantry, captured in Battle at Sailor's creek April 6th 1865. by Corporal J. F. Benjamin Co. M (Harris') Vol. Cavalry 1st Brigade 3rd Division Maj. Gen. Custar Commdg. E.W. *Returned 3/25/05. 280*

303.   *Louisiana* Battle Flag of the Washington Artillery captured in Battle of Appomattox Station April 8th 1865 by Private Barney Shields Co. E. 2nd Virginia Cavalry 3rd Brigade 3rd Division, General Custar Commdg. E.W. *Returned 3/25/05. 281*

304.   Rebel Flag, captured by Lieut. Thomas W. Custar A.D.C. at the Battle of Namozine Church Va. April 2nd 1865. E.W. *282*

305.   Rebel Flag, *283*

306.   Virginia State Colors, captured at the Battle of Sailor's Creek April 6th 1865 by Corporal Ernine C. Payne 2nd New York (Harris') Vet. Cavalry 1st Brigade 3rd Cav. Div. Maj. Gen'l Custar Commdg. E.W. *Returned 3/25/05. 284*

307.   Rebel Battle Flag, captured by Noel Shorgety Co. A. 61st New York Volunteers. E.W. *4th N. Carolina Returned 3/25/05. 285*

308.   Rebel Battle Flag, captured in Battle at Farms Cross Roads Virginia April 5th 1865 by Sergeant J.K. Piersol, Co. F 13th Ohio Cavalry 3rd Brigade 2nd Cavalry Division General Crook Commdg. E.W. Ord. office *286*

309.   Rebel Battle Flag, captured in Battle at Sailor's Creek April 6th 1865 by Corporal Absalom Jordan Co. A. 3rd Inda Vol. Cavalry. Escort to Headquarters 3rd Cavalry Division General Custar Commdg. E.W. *287*

310.   Rebel Battle Flag, captured by Sergt J. W. Winter 5th Mich. Vols. April 6th 1865 at Sailor's Creek. E.W. *(61 Virginia) Returned 3/25/05. 288*

311.   Battle Flag, of the 19th Mississippi, Mahone's Division Longstreet's Corps. E.W. *Returned 3/25/05. 289*

312.   Red Confederate Flag. E.W. *290*

313.   Rebel Battle Flag, captured April 20th 1865 near Petersburg Va. by Private Theodore Mitchel Co. C 61st Penn. Vols. 3rd Brigade 2nd Div. 6th Army Corps. E.W. *Returned 4/26 291*

314.   Rebel Battle Flag, capture in Battle of Sailor's Creek April 6th 1865 by Major John Allestron 3rd N.Y. Cav. Vols. 1st Brigade 3rd Cavalry Division Genl. Custar Commdg. E.W. *292*

315.   Rebel Battle Flag, captured at Sailor's Creek April 6th 1865 by Lieut. John R. Norton Co. M. 1st N.Y. Lincoln Cavalry 3rd Brigade 3rd Cavalry Division Gen. Custar Commdg. E.W. Ord. office *293*

316.   Rebel Battle Flag, captured in Battle at Sailor's Creek April 6th 1865 by S.P. Kenyon Co. B. 24th New York Cavalry, 1st Brigade, 2nd Cavalry Division, General Crook Commdg. E.W. *294*

317.   Rebel Flag, captured by Corpl. Elijah A. Briggs Co. B 2nd Conn. H.A. Vols. 2nd Brigade 1st Division 6th Corps at Petersburg Va. April 2nd 1865. E.W. Ord. office *295*

318.   Flag, captured at the Battle of Petersburg VA. April 2nd 1865 by Private Isaac James Co. A. 110th Ohio Vols. E.W. Ord. office *296*

319.   Rebel Flag, captured at Sailor's Creek, April 6th 1865 by Private John Chapman, 1st Maine Heavy Artillery. E.W. Ord. office *297*

320.   Head Quarters Flag of Brig. Genl. Barranger Commdg. North Carolina Brigade of Cavalry, captured by Wm. H. Woodall, Head Qrs Scout of General Sheridan, Residence Lynchburg Va. C *Returned 3/ 25/05. 298*

321.   Small Confederate Colors. Stars and Bars. C *299*

322.   Rebel Battle Flag, captured at the Battle of Five Forks April 1st 1865 by Lieut. W.W. Winnegar Co. B. 1st N.Y. Dragoons, 2nd Brig. 1st Cavalry Division Gen'l Devin Commdg. E.W. Ord. office *300*

323.   Rebel Flag, captured by Lewis F. Briser*[?]* Co. D. 57th Pa. Vet. Volunteers. C.W. Ord. office *301*

324.   Rebel Battle Flag, captured by Private Benjamin Gifford, Co. A 121st N.Y. Vols 2nd Brigade 1st Division 6th Corps in Battle of Little Sailor's Creek April 6th 1865. *June 26th 1865. Loaned to Col. E. Olcott 121st N.Y. , By order of the Secty of War. 302*

325.   Rebel Battle Flag, captured by Lieut. Thomas W. Custar A.D.C. at the Battle of Sailor's Creek Va. April 6th 1865. E.W. Ord. office *303*

326.   Rebel Battle Flag, captured in Battle at Sailor's Creek April 6th 1865 by Captain E. F. Savacoal Co. K 1st New York (Lincoln) Volunteer Cavalry 3rd Brigade 3rd Cavalry Division General Custar Commdg. E.W. *304*

327.   Battle Flag, of the 50th Georgia, captured by Corporal John Keough Co. E 67th Penn Vols at the Battle of Sailor's Creek Va. April 6th 1865. E.W. *Returned 3/25/05. 305*

328.   Rebel Flag, captured in Battle at Farm's Cross Roads April 5th 1865 by Sergeant Alexander C. Ellicott Co. A. 1st Penn Cavalry, 1st Brigade 2nd Cav. Division General Crook Commdg. E.W. Ord. office *306*

329.   Confederate Flag. E.W. *307*

330.   Rebel Battle Flag, captured at the Battle of Sailor's Creek, April 6th 1865 by Corp'l Walter L. Mundell, 5th Mich. Vols. E.W. *308*

331.   Rebel Battle Flag, captured by Private Charles A. Taggart Co. B. 37th Mass. Vols at the Battle of Sailor's Creek Va. April 6th 1865 3rd Brigade 3rd Cavalry Division 6th Army Corps. E.W. Ord. office *309*

332.   Rebel Battle Flag, of the 11th Florida Infantry captured in the Battle of Sailor's Creek VA. April 6th 1865 by 1st Lieut. A. F. Lamfire, Co. B 1st Conn. Cavalry 1st Brigade 3rd Cav. Division Gen'l Custar Commdg. E.W. Ord. office *Returned 3/25/05. 310*

333.   Battle Flag, of the 12th Va. Infantry, captured in the Battle of Sailor's Creek April 6th 1865 by Sergeant T. M. Cunningham Co. H 1st Va. Vet. Vol Cavalry, 3rd Brig. 3rd Cav. Division Gen'l Custar Commdg. E.W. *Returned 3/25/05. 311*

334.   Rebel Battle Flag, of 1st Texas Infantry, captured in Battle at Appomattox Station, April 8th 1865 by 1st Lieut. Martin A. Reed Co. D. 8th N.Y. Vols. 2nd Brigade 3rd Cav. Division General Geo. A. Custar Commdg. E.W. *Returned 4/26/05. 312*

335.   Rebel Battle Flag, captured in Battle of Farm's Cross Roads April 5th 1865 by Sergt John W. Davidsiger Co. A. 1st Penn Cav. 1st Brigade 2nd Division General Crook Commdg. E.W. Ord. office *313*

336.   Rebel Flag, captured in Battle at Sailor's Creek April 6th 1865 by Captain H. P. Boon, 1st Va. Vet. Vol. Cavalry 3rd Brigade 3rd Division General Custar Commanding. E.W. Ord. office *314*

337.   Rebel Flag, captured at Sailor's Creek April 6th 1865 by Corp'l Crustrim Connell Co. I 138th Pa Volunteers. E.W. Ord. office *Returned to Va. 4/26/05. 315*

338.   Battle Flag captured by Sergt Lister G. Hack Co. F. 5th Vermont Vols. 2nd Brigade 2nd Division 6th Corps. E.W. Ord. office *(23 Tenn?) Returned 4/26/05. 316*

339.   Battle Flag, of the Sumpter Heavy Artillery, captured in the Battle of Sailor's Creek, April 6th 1865 by Sergt. Geo. J. Pitman, Co. C. 1st N.Y. (Lincoln) Vol. Cavalry 3rd Brig. 3rd Division, General Custar Commanding. E.W. Ord. office *Returned 4/26/05. 317*

340.   Battle Flag, captured in the battle of Five Forks, April 1st 1865 by Lieut. H. G. Bonebrake Co. G. 17th Penn. Vols. Cav. 2nd Brig. 1st Cav. Division, General Thomas De Vise Commanding. E.W. Ord. office *318*

341.   Battle Flag, captured at the Battle of Sailor's Creek Va. April 6th 1865 by Serg't Wm. Holton Co. F. 1st Va. Vet Volunteers Cavalry 3rd Brig. 3rd Division General Custar Commanding. E.W. *24th Va. Inf. Returned 3/25/05. 319*

342.   Flag of the 46th Regiment North Carolina Vols. picked up on the Rebel line by Lieut. Brant of the 1st West Va. N.J. Volunteers. E.W. Ord. office *Returned 4/26/05. 320*

343.   Colors of the 7th Tennessee Regt. captured by Private Milton Mathew Co. C. 61st Reg't Penn. Vols. 3rd Brigade, 2nd Division, he also captured the Color Sergeant. E.W. Ord. office *321*

344.   Battle Flag, captured by Corp'l Miller Blickenderfer Co. E. 126th Ohio Vols. at the Battle of Petersburg Va. April 2nd 1865. E.W. *Returned 4/26/05 322*

345.   Confederate Standard, captured by Sergeant Wesley Gibbs Co. B. 2nd Conn. H.A. Vols at the Battle of Little Sailor's Creek April 6th 1865 2nd Brig. 1st Division 6th Corps. E.W. Ord. office *323*

346.   Battle Flag belonging to Fields Division Longstreet's Corps. E.W. Ord. office *324*

347.   Battle Flag of the 14th Alabama Regiment captured by Ed Hoary, Priv. Co. B 25th N.Y. Cav. at Winchester Va Sept. 19/64 Samuel Cassady 1 U.S. Cavy assisted in capture Information acc'd from Wm. D. Campbell late of 25 NY Cavy P.O. 464 Manor Street Columbia Pa E.W.

Returned 3/25/05. *325*

348.   Battle Flag. E.W. Ord office *326*

349.   Battle Flag. of the 6th Tennessee Infantry captured in Battle of Sailor's Creek April 6th 1865 by Sergeant Waller F. McWhorten Co. E 3rdWest Virginia Cavalry 3rd Brig. 3rd Div, General Custar Commdg. E.W. *Returned 3/25/05.* *327*

350.   Battle Flag. Virginia State Colors, captured in Battle at Farms Cross Roads April 5th 1865 by Henry C Wasfel Co. A 1st Penn. Cavalry, 1st Brigade 2nd Cav. Division, Bvt. Maj. Gen. Crook Commanding. E.W. Ord. office *Returned 3/25/05.* *328*

351.   Battle Flag. E.W. *329*

352.   Battle Flag, captured in Battle at Farms Cross Roads, April 5th 1865 by Sergeant George W.Stewart Co. E 1st N.J. Cavalry 1st Brigade, 2nd Cav. Division, General Crook Commanding. C. *330*

353.   Battle Flag of Sumpter Flying Artillery, captured in the Battle of Appomattox Station April 8th 1865 by Chief Bugler Charles Sharn 1st Va Vet. Vol. Cavalry 3rd Brigade 3rd Cav. Division. General Custar Commanding. E.W. Ord. office *Returned 4/26/05.* *331*

354.   Colors of the 47th Regiment North Carolina Vols, captured by Private Joseph Phillips Co. E 148th Penn Vols. April 2nd 1865 at Sutherland Station. E.W. *Returned 3/25/05.* *332*

355.   Battle Flag of the 18th Fla. Infty captured in battle at Sailor's Creek April 6th 1865 by Private Daniel Woods Co. K 1st Va. Vet Vol. Cavalry 3rd Brigade 3rd Cav. Division General Custar Commanding. E.W. Ord. office *Returned 3/25/05/* *334*[sic]

356.   Battle Flag captured in Battle of Appomattox Station, April 8th 1865 by Corp'l Thomas Anderson Co. I 1st West Va. Vet. Vol. Cav. 3rd Brigade 2nd Division General Custar Commanding. E.W. Ord. office *335*

357.   Battle Flag of the 6th N.C. Infty captured in Battle of Sailor's Creek April 6th 1865 by Private Joseph Kimball Co. B 2nd West Va. Vol. Cav. 3rd Brigade 3rd Cavalry Division General Custar Commanding. E.W. Ord. office *Returned 3/25/05.* *336*

358.   Battle Flag captured in Battle of Sailor's Creek April 6th 1865 by Private Samuel A. McElhring Co. A. 2nd Va. Cav. 3rd Brig. 3rd Cav.

Division. General Custar Commanding. E.W. *337*

359.   Battle Flag captured in battle at Sailors Creek April 6th 1865 by Captain E. M. Miller Co. C. 1st Conn. Cav. Vols. 1st Brigade 3rd Division General Custar Commanding. E.W. Ord. office *338*

360.   Battle Flag of the 40th Va Infty, captured in Battle of Sailors Creek April 6th 1865 by 1st Sergt. W.P. Morris Co. C. 1st N.Y. (Lincoln) Cavalry Vols. 3rd Brigade 3rd Division General Custar Commdg. E.W. *Returned 3/25/05. 339*

361.   Battle Flag captured in Battle of Farms Cross Roads, April 5th 1865 by Sergt. A.J. Young Co. F. 1st Penn. Cav. 1st Brigade 3rd Div. General Crook Commandg. E.W. *340*

362.   This Flag was captured by Corp'l. Chas. Marguette Co. F 93rd Penn. Vols. 1st Brigade, 2nd Division 6th Corps. F.R. Ord. office *341*

363.   Battle Flag of the 26th Va. Infantry, captured in Battle of Sailor's Creek April 6th 1865 by Coran D. Evans Co. A. 3rd Inda Vet. Cav. Escort to Headquarters 3rd Cav. Div. General Custar Commandg. E.W. Ord. office *Returned 3/25/05. 342*

364.   Battle Flag of the 28th North Carolina Reg't Wilcox Division. E.W. *Returned 3/25/05. 343*

365.   Battle Flag of the 14th Georgia Reg't Heth's Division Longstreet's Corps. E.W. *Returned 3/25/05. 344*

366.   Battle Flag E.W. Ord. office *345*

367.   Remnant of Battle Flag. N *346*

368.   Battle Flag, Heath's Division Longstreet's Corps N *347*

369.   Battle Flag captured at the Battle of Sailor's Creek April 6th 1865 by Private Henry Hoffman Co. M 2nd Ohio Vet. Volunteers 1st Brig. 3rd Cav. Division, General Custar Commanding. N *348*

370.   Remnant of a Battle Flag. N *349*

371.   Remnant of a Battle Flag. C.W. *350*

372.   Battle Flag of the 18th Va Infantry, captured in Battle at Sailor's Creek April 6th 1865 by 1st Serg't. *Iven S. Calking* Co. M 2nd New York (Harris Light Cavalry) 1st Brigade 3rd Cavalry Division, Bvt.

Maj. Genl. Geo. A. Custar Commdg. N *Returned 3/25/05. 351*

373.   Battle Flag captured by Serg't <u>J. Donalson</u> Co. I 4th Penn. Cavalry near Appomattox C.H. Va. April 9th 1865. N. *Returned to VA., 4/26/05. 352*

374.   <u>Rebel Battle Flag</u> N *353*

375.   Battle Flag of Picket's Division Longstreet's Corps. N *Returned to Va. 4/26/05. 354*

376.   <u>Battle Flag</u> of Mahone's Division, Longstreet's Corps. N *355*

377.   <u>Battle Flag</u> of Heth's Division, Longstreet's Corps. N *356*

378.   <u>Battle Flag</u>. N.W. *357*

379.   <u>Battle Flag</u> taken from Gordon's Division. N.W. *358*

380.   <u>Staff and Remnant of Flag.</u> N.W. *359*

381.   <u>Battle Flag</u> of Field's Division Longstreet's Corps. N.W. *360*

382.   <u>Remnant of Battle Flag</u>. N.W. *361*

383.   <u>Battle Flag of Gordon's Corps.</u> N.W. *(12th Virginia)* N.W. *Returned 3/25/05. 362*

384.   <u>Battle Flag</u>, captured by Corporal <u>Richard Welch</u> Co. E. 37th Mass. Vols 3rd Brigade 1st Division 6th Corps. N.W. *363*

385.   Battle Flag of the 18th N.C. captured near Petersburg Va. April 2nd 1865 by Private <u>Frank Frey</u> Co. A 40th N.Y. Vols. N.W. Ord. office *Returned 3/25/05. 364*

386.   <u>Battle Flag</u> Field's Division Longstreet's Corps. N.W. *365*

387.   <u>Confederate Standard</u>, Stars and Bars, captured in Battle of Appomattox Station, April 8th 1865 by Saddler <u>J.E. Sova*[?]*</u> Co. H. 8th N.Y. Cav. Vols. 2nd Brig. 3rd Division, General Custar Commdg. N.W. *366*

388.   <u>Battle Flag</u>. N.W. Ord. office *367*

389.   <u>Battle Flag</u>, captured in Battle of Farm's Cross Roads, April 5th 1865 by Private <u>George W. Schinal</u> Co. M. 24th N.Y. Cavalry, 1st

Brigade 2nd Division General Crook Commdg. N.W. Ord. office *368*

390.   Battle Flag. N.W. Ord. office *369*

391.   Battle Flag captured by Corporal Chas. Deloff Co. K 11th Vermont Vols. 2nd Brigade 2nd Div. 6th Corps. He captured the Flag by making the Color bearer surrender. (The Flag is mutilated on account of the bearer seeing our rapid advance, tore the Flag from the Staff and was prevented from tearing it to pieces, by the quick movements of Corporal Deloff.) N.W. *Mississippi — Returned 4/26/05. 370*

392.   Battle Flag of the 48th Alabama, Fields Division, Longstreet's Corps. N.W. Ord. office *Returned 3/25/05. 371*

393.   Battle Flag. N.W. Ord. office *372*

394.   Battle Flag, Fields Division, Longstreet's Corps. N.W. Ord. office. *373*

395.   Battle Flag of Mahone's Division, Longstreet's Corps. N.W. Ord. office *374*

396.   Battle Flag of Mahone's Division, Longstreet's Corps. N.W. Ord. office *375*

397.   Battle Flag. C *376*

398.   Battle Flag of Gordon's Corps. N.W. Ord. office *377*

399.   Battle Flag of the 7th Georgia Regiment. N.W. Ord. office *Returned 3/25/05. 378*

400.   Battle Flag of the 38th N. C. Wilcox's Division, Longstreet's Corps. N.W. Ord. office *Returned 3/25/05. 379*

401.   Battle Flag. N.W. Ord. office *380*

402.   Confederate Colors. Stars and Bars. N.W. Ord. office *381*

403.   Battle Flag of Gordon's Corps. N.W. Ord. office *382*

404.   Battle Flag of Mahone's Division, Longstreet's Corps. N.W. Ord. office *383*

405.   Battle Flag of the 41st Va. Infantry, Weisiger's Brig. Mahone's Div. N.W. Ord. office *Returned 3/25/05. 384*

406.   <u>Battle Flag.</u> N.W. Ord. office *385*

407.   <u>Battle Flag</u>. Field's Division, Longstreet's Corps. N.W. *386*

408.   <u>Battle Flag.</u> N.W. *387*

409.   <u>Battle Flag</u>, Mahone's Division, Longstreet's Corps. N.W. *388*

410,   <u>Battle Flag</u>, of the 8th Florida Infantry, captured in Battle of Sailor's Creek April 6th 1865 by 1st Serg't A. A. Clapp, Co. G. 2nd Ohio Vet. Vol. Cavalry 1st Brig. 3rd Cav. Div. General Custar Commdg. N.W. *Returned 3/25/05. 389*

411.   <u>Battle Flag</u>, of Fields Div. Longstreet's Corps. (Remarks on paper pasted on staff) "Mr. Yankee you will please return this Flag staff and shoulder belt over to the 9th Maine, was captured at St. Gilmore on the 29th October 1864. by the 3rd Forks Reg't Vols" (Signed) "Big Rebel" N.W. Ord. office *390*

412.   <u>Battle Flag</u>. N.W. Ord. office *391*

413.   <u>Battle Flag</u> of the 31st Georgia, Gordon's Corps. N.W. Ord. office *Returned 3/25/05 392*

414.   <u>Battle Flag</u> of the 2nd Florida. N.W. Ord. office *Returned 3/25/05. 393*

415.   <u>Battle Flag</u>, Heth's Division Longstreet's Corps. N.W. Ord. office *394*

416.   <u>Battle Flag</u>. N.W. Ord. office *395*

417.   <u>Battle Flag</u>. N.W. Ord. office *396*

418.   <u>Battle Flag</u>. N.W. Ord. office *397*

419.   <u>Battle Flag</u>. Field's Division Longstreet's Corps. N.W. Ord. office *398*

420.   <u>Confederate Colors</u>, "Stars and Bars" belonging to the 34th N.C. Wilcox Division, Longstreet's Corps. N.W. Ord. office *Returned 3/25/05. 399*

421.   <u>Battle Flag</u> C Ord. office *400*

422.   Battle Flag. N.W. Ord. office *401*

423.   Battle Flag. Gordon's Corps. N.W. Ord. office *402*

424.   Battle Flag Taken from Longstreet's Corps. N.W. Ord. office *403*

425.   Battle Flag. N.W. Ord. office *404*

426.   Battle Flag of the 25th Batt. Va Infantry, captured in Battle at Sailor's Creek, April 6th 1865 by Private Frank Miller Co. M 2nd New York (Harris' Light) Vol. Cav. 1st Brigade 3rd Cav. Division General Custar Commdg. N.W. Ord. office *Returned 3/25/05. 405*

427.   Battle Flag of the 49th Georgia N.W. Ord. office *Returned 3/25/05. No history 406*

428.   Battle Flag of the 13th N.C. Wilcox Division, Longstreet's Corps. N.W. Ord. office *Returned 3/25/05. 407*

429.   Flag of the 60th Georgia Gordon's Corps. N.W. Ord. office *Returned 3/25/05. 408*

430.   Battle Flag. Gordon's Corps. N.W. Ord. office *409*

431.   Battle Flag of Wilcox's Division, Longstreet's Corps. N.W. Ord. office *410*

432.   Battle Flag. Mahone's Division, Longstreet's Corps. N.W. Ord. office *411*

433.   Battle Flag, Wilcox's Division, Longstreet's Corps. N.W. Ord. office *no history 412*

434.   Battle Flag of the 30th North Carolina. N.W. Ord. office N.W. Ord. office *Returned 3/25/05. 413*

435.   Battle Flag of the 45th Georgia, Heth's Division, Longstreet's Corps. N.W. Ord. office *Returned 3/25/05 414*

436.   Battle Flag, Mahone's Division, Longstreet's Corps. N.W. Ord. office *415*

437.   Battle Flag 12th Va. Infty. captured in Battle at Sailor's Creek April 6th 1865 by 1st Lieut. James H. Gibben Co. C. 2nd New York (Harris' Light) Vol. Cav. 1st Brig. 3rd Div. General Custar Commdg.

N.W. Ord. office *416*

438.   Battle Flag. C. Ord. office *417*

439.   Marker, captured April 2nd 1865 near Petersburg, Va. by Sergt. Frank Schubert Co. E 43rd N.Y. Vols. 3rd Brig. 2nd Division 6th Corps. N.W. Ord. office *418*

440.   Marker, captured April 2nd 1865 near Petersburg, Va. by Sergt. Frank Schubert Co. E 43rd N.Y. Vols. 3rd Brig. 2nd Division 6th Corps. N.W. Ord. office *419*

441.   Remnant of a Rebel Flag. N.W. Ord. office *420*

442.   Battle Flag captured Feb. 6th 1865 in engagement near Hatcher's Run, by Sergt. David Caldwill Co. H. 13th Penn. Cavalry (Signed) D.M.M. Gregg Bvt. Maj. Gen'l Vols. Com. Division C *421*

443.   This Flag was captured at Columbus, Ga. April 16th 1865 by Corpl. Richard H. Morgan, Co. A 4th Iowa Cavalry 1st Brigade 4th Division Cav. Corps, M.D.M. Inside the line of works during the charge. The bearer contested with the Corporal for its possession. Upton's Division, Winslow's Brigade (sent to the state of Iowa by order of the Secretary of War.) A. *422*

444.   This Flag was captured by Private John H. Hays Co. F 4th Iowa Cav. 1st Brigade 4th Div. Cav. Corps M.D.M. at Columbus, Ga. April 16th 1865. Private Hays captured the Standard and Bearer, who tore it from the staff and tried to escape, firing his revolver, and wounding one man, belonging to the 4th Iowa Cavalry
        (Upton's Division Winslow's Brigade) (Sent to the state of Iowa by order of the Sect'y of War) *Sent to the State of Iowa by order of the Secretary of War*

445.   Rebel Flag, captured at Blakely, Ala. April 7th 1865 by Lieut Col. Victor Vilguain 97th Illinois. C. Ord. office *423*

446.   Rebel Flag, captured at Blakely, Ala. April 9th 1865 by Captain Samuel McConnell, Co. H, 119th Illinois Ord. office *424*

447.   Rebel Flag, captured at Blakely, Ala. April 9th 1865 by Capt. Henry A. Miller Co. B 8th Illinois. C. Ord. office *425*

448,   Rebel Flag, captured at Blakely, Ala. April 9th 1865 by 1st Serg't. Joseph Stickler Co. A. 83rd Ohio. N.W. Ord. office *426*

449.   *2nd Ala Inf.* Rebel Flag, captured by Serg't. Geo. F. Robinson, Co. B 119th Ill. Vols. at Balkely Ala. April 9th 1865. C Ord. office *Returned 3/25/05. 427*

450.   Rebel Flag, captured at Spanish Fort, Ala. April 8th 1865 by Serg't. Edgar A. Bras Co. K 8th Iowa. C. *428*

451.   Rebel Flag, captured at Blakely Ala. April 9th 1865 by Private John H. Gallahan Co. B 122nd Ill. Vols. C *429*

452.   Rebel Flag, captured at Blakely Ala. April 9th 1865 by Private John Whitmore Co. F. 119th Ill. Vols. C. *430*

453.   *Ala* Rebel Flag, near Blakely, Ala April 4th 1865 by Private Thomas Riley, Co. D 1st La. Cavalry (captured) NW Ord Office *431*

454.   Rebel Flag, found by men of the 3rd Division 16th A.C. after the capture of Spanish Fort, Ala April 9th 1865. C Ord. office *432*

455.   Rebel Flag, found by men of the 3rd Division 16th A.C. after the capture of Spanish Fort, Ala April 9th 1865. N.W. Ord. office *433*

456.   *39 N.C. I.* Rebel Flag, found by men of the 3rd Division 16th A.C. after the capture of Spanish Fort, Ala April 9th 1865. C. Ord. office *Returned 3/25/05. 434*

457.   This Flag, was captured one hundred yards from the bridge at Georgia, April 16th 1865, by Private Edmund J. Bibb Co. D 4th Iowa Cav. 1st Brig. 4th Division cavalry corps M.D.M. The enemy ran from our men leaving the flag. Upton's Division—Winslow Brigade C. *435*

458.   This Flag, with the bearer was captured in the streets at Columbia, Ga. April 16th 1865 by Serg't Norman F. Bates, Co. E 4th Iowa Cav. 1st Brig., 4th Division Cav. Corps. M.D.M. Upton's Division, Winslow's Brigade. C *Returned 3/25/05. 436*

458 "A". This Flag belonged to the 10th Mo. Battery, was captured with its bearer at Columbus, Ga. April 16th 1865. by Private John Kinney, 4th Iowa Cavalry 1st Brigade 4th Div. Cav. Corps M.D.M. by Private Kinney had a struggle with its bearer for its possession. Upton's Division, Winslow's Brigade. C. *Returned 3/25/05. 437*

459.   This Flag, belonged to the 12th Miss. Cavy. and was captured with its bearer at Selma Ala. April 2nd 1865 by Private James P. Miller Co. D 4th Iowa Cavalry 1st Brig. 4th Div. Cav. Corps M.D.M. Upton's Division Winslow's Brigade. N.W. Ord. office *Returned 3/25/05. 438*

460.   *11 Mississippi* This Flag with its bearer, was captured at Selma, Ala. April 2nd 1865 by Pvt. Chas. A. Swan Co. K 4th Iowa Cav. 1st Brigade 4th Division Cav. Corps. M.D.M. The bearer stated it belonged to the 11th Mississippi. Upton's Div. Winslow's Brigade. N.W. Ord. office *Returned 3/25/05. 439*

461.   This Flag, was captured at Columbus Ga. April 16th 1865 on the west end of the bridge by Private Richard H. Cogsriff Co. L 4th Iowa Cavalry 1st Brig. 4th Div. Cav. Corps, M.D.M. Private Cogsriff knocked the bearer down with his carbine before he could obtain possession of it. Upton's Division, Winslow's Brigade. A.B. *440*

462.   Rebel Flag plain white P *441*

463.   Rebel Signal Flag blue and white. C. Ord. office *442*

464.   Rebel Signal Flag 1st Repeater. C. Ord. office *443*

465.   Rebel Signal Flag red and white. C. Ord. office *444*

466.   Rebel Signal Flag 2nd Repeater. C. Ord. office *445*

467.   Rebel Flag resembles English Union Jack F.R. *446*

468.   Rebel Flag captured on a train at the R. R. Depot in Macon Ga. by Private Ruben Phillips Co. C 17th Indiana Vol Infantry 1st Brigade 2nd Division Cavalry Corps M.D.M. Long's Division, Millers Division. C. Ord. office *X is this correct R 447*

469.   Rebel Flag was captured by Buford's Brigade, and was captured by the 7th Kentucky in a gallant charge against double its number, near Montgomery, Ala. April 12th 1865 2nd Brigade 1st Div. Cav. Corps M.D.M. McCook's Division, Lagrange's Brigade C Ord. office *448*

470.   Rebel Flag Red and White. C. Ord. office *449*

471.   Confederate Standard. C. *450*

472.   *Louisiana* Rebel Flag Belonged to Austins Battery, was captured at Columbus, Georgia April 16th 1865, with its bearer, by Private Andrew Tibbitts, 3rd Iowa Cavalry 1st Brigade 4th Division Cavalry Corps M.D.M. inside the line of works and to the right of the 4 gun Battery on the right of the enemy's line. Upton's Division Winslow's Brigade C. Ord. office *Returned 3/25/05. 451*

473.   Rebel Signal Flag answering. C. Ord. office _452_

474.   Rebel Streamer. C. Ord. office _453_

475.   Rebel Signal Flag. meal. C. Ord. office _454_

476.   Rebel Flag, captured with its bearer by Serg't. H.L. Birdsall, Co. B 3rd Iowa Cav. 1st Brigade 4th Division Cav. Corps M.D.M. near Columbus Ga. April 16th 1865 while his Company was assaulting the works on the left of the Summerville Road. Upton's Division: Winslow's Brigade. S.E.D. Ord. office _455_

477.   Rebel Signal Flag "Preparatory. C. _456_

478.   Signal Flag, "3rd Repeater." C. Ord. office _457_

479.   Signal Flag, "Interogatory." C. Ord. office _458_

480.   Signal Flag, "Church" C. Ord. office _459_

481.   Streamer. C. Ord. office _460_

482.   Signal Flag "Guard" F.R. _461_

483.   Bonnie Blue Flag. C. _462_

484.   Rebel Flag of the General Jackson captured by the 1st Brigade 4th Division C.C. at Columbus Ga. April 16th 1865. C. _463_

485.   Rebel Flag Blue yellow and Red. W.W. _464_

486.   Rebel Flag yellow and Blue. C. _465_

487.   Rebel Flag of the Dixie Rangers captured by a detachment of the 4th Ind'a Cav. in skirmish near Barnesville Ga. April 19th 1865 2nd Brig. 1st Division Cav. Corps. McCook's Division Lagranger's Brigade C. Ord. office _466_

488.   _Georgia_ Rebel Flag belonging to the "Worrill Grays" captured near Culloden Ga. by Private A.B. Hudson and J. Davis, 17th Ind'a Mounted Infty 1st Brig. 2nd Div. Cav. Corps. M.D.M. during a smart skirmish in which a small party of the 17th Ind'a routed two hundred Militia May 20th 1865. Long's Division Millers Brigade C. _Returned 3/25/05_ _467_

489.   This Flag was surrendered at Macon, Ga. by Col. Cummings

C.S.A. to <u>Lieut. McDowell</u> 17th Ind'a Mounted Inft'y. 1st Brigade 2nd Division Cavalry Corps. This city was surrendered without resistance. May 20th 1865. Long's Division, Millers C *468*

490.   <u>Signal Flag,</u> Cornet C. Ord. office *469*

491.   <u>Battle Flag</u> captured from the Rebels at Hatcher's Run, Va. April 2nd 1865 by Serg't <u>Adam White</u> Co. G. 11th West Va. Vols. C *470*

492.   <u>Rebel Flag</u> of the 12th Miss. Cavalry captured near Tuskega Ala. by Private <u>John H. Shouf</u> Co. H 3rd Ohio Cavalry 2nd Brigade 2nd Division Cav. Corps. M.D.M. Private Shouf captured Major Box, commanding the above Regiment at the same time. Long's Division Mintry's Brigade. *Returned 3/25/05* S.E.C. *471*

493.   <u>Garrison Flag</u> of Fort Tyler, Ga. captured in the assault upon the Fort at West Point, Ga. by detachment from 1st Wis. 2nd Ind'a and 7th Kentucky Cavalry, 2nd Brig. 1st Div. Cav. Corps. M.D.M. The 1st Wis. was first inside the fort and lost twice as many men in the battle as both the other detachments. McCook's Division, Lagranger's Brigade. S.E.C. *472*

494.   <u>Flag</u> captured by General A.L. Lee's Cavalry Command at Camp Moore, La. on the N.O and Jackson Railroad. S.E.C. *473 (see no. 172 list of U.S. Flags)*

495.   *Florida* <u>Flag of the Appalachacola Guards</u>. F.R. *Returned 3/ 25/05. 474*

496.   <u>Rebel Battle Flag</u> captured at Sailor's Creek April 6th 1865 by <u>E.M. Norton</u> Adjutant 6th Mich. Cavalry 1st Brig. 1st Cav. Div. General Devin Commanding. N.W. Ord. office *475*

497.   <u>Rebel Flag</u>, captured by Serg't <u>F.M. McMillen</u> Co. C 110th Ohio Vols. at the Battle of Petersburg Va. April 2nd 1865. F.R. *476*

498.   <u>Chief Engineer's Flag</u> Army of Northern Virginia captured April 4th 1865 by <u>William J. Brewer</u> Gen'l Sheridan's Hdqr Scout. Residence, Orange Co. N.Y. (Co. C 2nd N.Y. Cavalry) F.R. *477*

499.   *44th Tenn.* <u>Rebel Battle Flag</u>, (silk) captured at Sailor's Creek April 6th 1865 by <u>E. M. Norton</u>, Adj 6th Mich. Cav. 1st Brig 1st Cav. Division, General Devin Commdg. A.C. *Returned 4/26/05. 478*

500.   *6th Ark. Vols.* <u>Rebel Flag</u> captured by Serg't <u>John W. Dean</u> Co. C. 17th Ind'a Vols. at Macon, Georgia. F.R. *Returned 3/25/05. 479*

501.   Rebel Flag, captured during the assault on Selma Ala. April 2nd 1865 by the Staff of Brig. Gen'l. Ely Long Commanding 2nd Div. Cav. Corps. A Ord. office _480_

502.   Rebel Flag, captured by Warren Dockum, Private Co. H. 121st N.Y. Vols. in the engagement at Sailor's Creek, April 6th 1865. Inscription: "For Our Altars and Our Hearths" "Savanna Vols Guards 1862" _Loaned to Col. Olcott 121st N.Y. Vols. by order of Sect'y of War_

503.   Garrison Flag, "Secessionville" James Island S.C. Defences of Charleston captured February 1865. Presented to the War Department by Brig. Gen'l A. Schimmelfennig. C. _Returned 4/26/05._ _481_

504.   Garrison Flag "Fort Moultrie" Charleston Harbor captured February 18th 1865. Presented to the War Department by Brig. Gen'l. A. Schimmelfennig. S.E.C. _Returned 4/26/05._ _482_

505.   Garrison Flag, Fort Ripley Charleston Harbor, S.C. captured February 18th 1865. Presented to the War Department by Brig. Gen'l. A. Schimmelfennig. W.W. Ord. office _Returned 4/26/05._ _483_

506.   Rebel Flag, found in a Blockade Runner, at Wilmington, N.C. February 22nd 1865. Deposited by Major S.N. Litchen Chief of Cavalry, Department of N.C. July 31st 1865. E.W. _484_

507.   United States Flag recaptured from the Rebel authorities by the forces of Major General Schofield, in the State of N.C. during the month of April 1864._[1865]_ Captured by the 9th Reg't. Tenn. Cavalry (Col. Biffles), at Resaca, Ga. May 15th 1864. No. 144- List of U.S. Flags. _See 144 Union Flags_ C. _485_

508.   Garrison Flag of the Citadel of Charleston S.C. captured February 18th 1865. Presented to the War Department by Brig. Gen'l. A. Schimmelfennig. C. _Returned 4/26/05._ _486_

509.   Garrison Flag of Castle Thunder. A _487_

510.   Garrison Flag of Castle Pinckney, captured February 18th 1865. Presented to the War Department by Brig. General A. Schimmelfennig. C. _Returned 4/26/05._ _488_

511.   Garrison Flag of Fort Fisher on case _489_

512.   Storm Flag captured at Savannah by the 2nd Div. 20th Corps Dec. 21st 1864. S.E.C. _490_

513.   <u>Storm Flag</u>, captured at Savannah. S.E.C. *491*

514.   <u>Storm Flag</u> captured at Savannah. S.W. Ord. office *492*

515.   <u>Rebel Flag</u> Virginia Inscribed "our cause is just, our rights we will maintain." *N.L.A.B.* W.W. *Returned 3/25/05.* 493

516.   <u>Captured by Corp'l Charles Shambaugh</u> Co. B 11th Penn Reserves at the Battle of Charles City Cross Roads June 30th 1862. W.W. Ord. office *494*

517.   <u>A Brigade Flag</u> belonging to the Third Division, 23rd Army Corps, picked up on the Field by the 16th Kentucky. Vols. See No. 198. List of U.S. Flags. W.W. Ord. office *495*

518.   <u>Scraps of a Union Regimental Flag</u>. History unknown. N.W.

519. & 520   <u>Sample Guidons</u> U.S.A. Sent by Col. G. H. Crosman Request of Quartermaster General Philadelphia. F.R. *(See No. 140 List of U.S. Flags)*

521.   *Ala.* <u>Rebel Battle</u> Flag captured by Private <u>P. Murphy</u> Co. K. 5th Ohio Vols. at the Battle of Antietam Sept. 17th 1862. C. *Returned 4/26/05. 496*

522.   <u>Colors</u> (union) captured by Private <u>Al Griffin,</u> Co. A. Shank's Regt. Mo. Cavalry, Shelby's Brigade at the battle of Marks' Hill April 25th 1864. Marmaduke's Division Mo. Cavalry. Not known how recaptured. C. *301*

523.   <u>Guidon</u>, captured from the Rebels by Corporal <u>Frank Carr</u> Co. D. 124th O.V.I. at the Battle of Brentwood Hills Dec. 16th 1864. C. *See No. 142 List of U.S. Flags Out 302*

524.   <u>U.S. Flag</u> recaptured from the enemy at Fort Tyler, West Point, Georgia April 16th 1865 by the 1st Brig. 1st Div. Cav. Corps M.D.M. C *See No. 143 List of U.S. Flags   Out   303*

525.   <u>U.S. Colors</u> captured at Donaldsonville, June, 1863. Not known how recaptured. C. *See No. 136 List of U.S. Flags Out 304*

526.   <u>Battle Flag</u> of 5th Va Cavalry captured at Aldie Va. June 17th 18<u>63</u> by 1st Mass. Cavy. C. Ord. office *Returned 3/25/05.   497*

527.   <u>Flag of Rebel Pirate Schooner</u> "Dixie" of Baltimore. S.E.W. *498*

Out 305

528.   State Flag of the 14th Va. Cavalry of 1864. Inscribed: "God armeth the Patriot" on one side and the other Virginia State Arms, captured by Private J. F. Adams Co. D 1st Va. Cavalry, on the 12th of November 1864 in an engagement near Ninevah Va (Signed) W.H. Powell Brig. Gen'l Commdg. 2nd Cav. Division W.W. Ord. office *Returned 3/25/05. 499*

529.   Rebel Flag swallow tail with blue cross in center, captured by Corporal James W. Parks, Co. F 11th Mo. Infantry at the Battle of Brentwood Hills near Nashville Tenn. C. *500*   *306*

530.   Rebel Flag of the 11th S.C. Volunteers. Inscribed: "Port Royal, Cedar Creek, Swift Creek, Petersburg June 24th. Weldon Rail Road. C. *Returned 3/25/05.*   *501*

531.   Battle Flag of the 6th and 7th Arkansas, captured by Private Henry B. Mattingly Co. E 10th Reg't Ky. Vols. 3rd Brig. 3rd Div. 14th Army Corps Army of the Cumberland Jonesboro Sept. 1st 1864. C. *Returned 3/25/05.*   *502*

532.   Confederate Guidon, captured by Private Daniel J. Holcomb Co. A 41st Ohio V. V. Infty. at the Battle of Brentwood Hills Dec. 16 1864. Army of the Cumberland. C. *503*   *307*

533.   Captured by the 1st Cav. Division, Department of the Cumberland, raid on Macon and Atlanta railroad, July 29th 1864. *Inscribed: "our Country and our rights." F.R. 504*   *308*

534.   Colors of the Clanton Alabama Brig. captured by the 2nd Ind'a Cavalry, 2nd Brigade 1st Division Cavalry Corps M.D.M.   near Montgomery, Ala. April 12th 1865. F.R. *Returned 3/25/05.* 505

535.   South Carolina State Flag, no history. F.R. *Returned May 1905.* 506

536.   Rebel Battle Flag, no history. C. *507*   *309*

537.   Rebel Battle Flag of the 1st Ark. Reg't. captured by the 14th Mich. Infantry near Jonesboro Georgia Sept. 1st 1864. C. Ord. office *Returned 3/31/05.* 508

538.   This Battle Flag was captured in the Battle at Wainsboro Va. March 2nd 1865. by Priv. C. Anderson Co. A 1st N. York Cavalry, 3rd Brig. 3rd Cav. Division, Bvt. Maj. General Geo. A. Custar Commdg. C.

509 *310*

539.   <u>Virginia Cavalry Standard</u>, taken in a charge at the battle of Williamsburg by Private <u>Samuel Caskey</u>, *Co. I 1st Cavalry.* Written with red ink (A.G.O.) 1862 N.W. *510*   *311*

540.   <u>Rebel Battle Flag</u> brought from Richmond by Master <u>Tad Lincoln</u> W.W. Ord. office *511 312*

541.   <u>Rebel Battle Flag</u>, no history. W.W. *512*   *313*

542.   <u>Rebel Battle Flag</u>, captured at Appomattox Court House, from the 46th Va. on the morning of April 9th, 1865, at 8.15 A.M. on the front line of battle by Col. West Funk Commdg. 121st Reg't Pa. Vols. and 142nd Pa. Vols in said engagement. These two Regiments were attached to the 3rd Brigade 3rd Division 5th Army Corps,-Army of the Potomac, General R. Coulter commanding Brigade, Gen'l Crawfords Division, General Griffin's Corps C. *513*   *314*

543.Total Rec'd 544 *Confederate battle flag captured from 17th and 18th Texas troops during the battle of Atlanta July 22 1864 by the 15 Mich Infty, left at War Dept. by Hon. W.F. Clark Aug. 27 1875 See 4567 Al 6 1875 Loaned to Gen'l W. T Clark, for use of a panorama about to be exhibited at Detroit Mich, by the authority of the Actg Secy War(See 333 AGO 1887) to be returned.*

544.   Conf. battle flag 17 Miss — Col. Holder (This flag is probably acctd for as "Confed Flag no history") *Returned 3/25/05.*

545.   Va. State flag presented by Lieut. E.D. Wheeler/Arty Nov. 1875 (This flag is probably acctd for as Confed. flag no history")

      As to number of confed. battle flags in custody of the War Dept: See 4037 AGO 1887. (also as to number of those captured in battle) 1 add'l 458(A)

      263 flags deposited in Ordnance museum. Returned to ago when Ordnance Museum was broken up. Deduct from total number of confed. flags Nos. 523, 524, & 525 — U.S. flags recaptured from confederates. Also Nos. 494—507—248—113— Total flags — (513) to be accounted for. 485 517 checked out

The first printing included the following errata:

No.	Error	Correction
38	48th Virginia	48th Georgia
45	July 3rd	July 2nd
50	1863	1862
72	7th Regt	9th Regt.
114	19th New York	79th New York
221	76th O.V.I.	96th O.V.I.
343	7th Louisiana	7th Tennessee
429	60th Virginia	60th Georgia
453	Priva	Private Thomas Riley, 1st Louisiana